Telling it slant

ALSO BY CHRIS CHIVERS
AND PUBLISHED BY PRETEXT
(unless otherwise stated)

Echoes of a Rainbow Song (1998, FB Press)
The Hard Road to Glory (2001)
The Open Window (2003)
Dear Dom and Greg ... (2007)
Jerusalem Haiku (2007)
South African Haiku (2008)
Blackburrn Cathedral (2010, Scala Publications)
Fully alive (2010)
From the belly of the whale (2012)

PHOTO: GREGORY CHIVERS

Telling it slant

Broadcasting faith in a contemporary world

Chris Chivers

edited Shuaib Karriem

PRETEXT
CAPE TOWN

In memoriam

DAVID ISITT

Friend, Scholar,
Priest, Pastor and Teacher

and for

VERITY ISITT

with much love and respect

Telling it slant: Broadcasting faith in a contemporary world
ISBN 978-0-9921940-0-0

*pre*Te**x**t ⊕

Pretext Publishers, P.O. Box 23199, Claremont 7735, South Africa
www.pretext.co.za   info@pretext.co.za

Contents

Foreword by The Reverend The Lord Griffiths of Burry Port

It's a delight to commend these radio sermons that have survived the transition from speech to print with amazing freshness and vigour. Chris Chivers, of course, has a great hinterland to draw upon. He's a musician and that's led me to be as intrigued by his musical material as by the sermons themselves. His experience of South Africa, Zimbabwe, Bosnia-Herzegovina, the Middle East and United States of America gives him a wealth of material to draw upon. So too does the work he did at Westminster Abbey, often in eye-catching moments of national importance, and also the cutting-edge work he undertook for five years with a Muslim colleague at Blackburn Cathedral. A preacher should always imagine himself holding the Bible in one hand and the daily newspaper in the other – his efforts should always be directed towards relating the ancient world to contemporary civilisation. Chris Chivers does this "in spades".

People don't speak well of preaching these days. The very verb "to preach" is taken to mean something akin to hectoring or moralising. Such perceptions are woefully wide of the mark. The modern preacher will remember only too well the old formula that defines his art as having three strands – persuasion, education and entertainment. It's an honourable craft and, well done, becomes an art form in its own right. A good modern preacher will have studied the "tricks of the trade" used by stand-up comedians and the producers of soap operas. He (or she) will have noted carefully how the attention of a viewer or listener is best retained by a succession of episodic incidents, asides and afterthoughts, which are layered on top of one another in quick succession. An occasional change of pace, a colourful illustration, an open-endedness in the delivery – all these factors can, taken together, produce a cocktail which can leave the listener both shaken and stirred. The sermon is the most underestimated yet powerful means of communication on the market today. As I read these efforts by Chris Chivers, I took great pleasure in the fact that the art of preaching is still very much alive and kicking.

I'm a Methodist – a follower of John Wesley who, in the 18th century decided to take the Good News of the gospel outside the ambit of the Church. He preached wherever he got a hearing – in market squares, in public halls, at crossroads, under trees or in the fields. I'm convinced that, were he alive today, he'd choose the air waves rather than the open-air. And he'd find a way to make a compelling case for the attractiveness of religion and the timelessness of its challenge. And that's what Chris Chivers seems to have achieved.

I've been contributing to Radio 4's Daily Service since 1987. Radio, unlike television, remains such a personal medium. Somehow, even when conducting an act of corporate worship, the preacher becomes a friend to his listeners. They, after all, are hearing him in the privacy of their own homes. I've become aware of the consolation I've given quite unwittingly to many a struggling soul listening to my efforts. And so, as a fellow practitioner, I applaud the decision to put what follows into print. I'm sure these sermons will be uplifting, stimulating, comforting and challenging to many a reader.

Introduction

All worship or liturgy – call it what we will – is an assertion of narrative. In a post-modern age where consumers are encouraged in the belief that any and every story is of value, worship re-asserts the timeless importance of engaging with one particular narrative that has proved its worth.

It proclaims that 'this story' is something to get to know, to probe, even to interrogate and certainly to inhabit because it has over-arching or under-girding qualities that can enhance life for all. It does not exclude the insights of other such 'meta-narratives' – indeed it seeks conversation with them. But it does assert that to understand the framework of life you can't be any and every-where, you have to start somewhere.

For 85 years, since 1928 – which makes it the longest-running broadcast radio programme in the world – Daily Service, and the Friday Act of Worship, on what is now BBC Radio 4 has for fifteen minutes each morning made such an assertion. It has provided a pause for reflection, a chance for the religiously inclined or inquisi-tive or even agnostic to (re)discover the heart of the faith tradition that has most shaped pre-modern, modern and post-modern Britain.

It's not an exclusive slot, either in terms of those who present it – who are from the widest spectrum of Christian denominations – or in terms of its 'free-preached' content – which allows wide scope for the Christian tradition to be brought into dialogue with any and every other world view. But it is nonetheless a resolutely Christian slot. I hesitated to use that phrase because it's so often taken to mean some protected sectarian space for the religiously narrow and misguided, of whom we have, if we're honest, rather too many for comfort in our twenty-first century world. But any-one who's ever listened to the Daily Service will know that this is not what its fifteen minute format is all about. A word about the format, because it made me somewhat hesitant in responding to the request for this book from many listeners who were kind enough to write appreciatively, some of them making the suggestion directly. The daily 9:45-9:59:50 slot – lest the presenter crash into the famous pips signalling that the time is 10:00 – is divided almost equally between spoken word and music. My hesitancy – not least, as a trained musician – comes in reproducing the words without the music that so deepens their frame of reference. The genre is also a broadcast medium. That's how it's meant to be experienced. Would it translate well in printed form? When I tried and made no adjustments to the 'spoken style' of the scripts it seemed to do so.

In setting the scripts out as I have I also realised more acutely the fact that the format is – as I hinted earlier – in essence a free-preached sermon in which all the elements combine to offer good news, a gospel even, in response to the bleakest contexts in the day's news.

People don't often produce books of sermons nowadays but they used to and perhaps – given the much briefer nature of these 'sermons' – here was a venture worth pursuing. It was not without precedent since on the occasion of the 70th anniversary of Daily Service Lavinia Byrne edited *The Daily Service Prayer Book (1998)* which contained a similar selection of 'scripts'.

As in the worship of all the mainline churches which follow lectionaries of readings, Daily Service presenters have to respond to a daily reading and a weekly theme that's set and I've indicated these themes in the title of each broadcast and printed the readings in full because I believe that if you simply reference them people never look them up! Writing their scripts, presenters must also respond to music that's carefully chosen to reflect the theme and the nuance each day's biblical passage gives to it. The whole process demands what all liturgy and worship demand – but which, amidst the fragmentation of post-modernism, they so rarely achieve – namely, coherence. This is what, I trust, readers will find.

The Daily Service stands or falls on its ability to communicate – that's the essence of broadcasting. But it's also the essence of Christianity whose central claims pertain to a supreme act of divine self-communication in Jesus Christ which Christians call the Incarnation. This 'communication' is the Christian model. There is no other.

This brings me to my title for this collection of fifty of the Daily Services I've been privileged to present over the last few years:

Telling it slant.

As you may already have discerned, I have a strong aversion to in-your-face 'Christianity direct' – the kind that Richard Dawkins rightly hates but wrongly supposes to be the only sort of Christianity around. I long ago learnt – when a formative influence, John Tinsley, then bishop of Bristol, introduced me – a small chorister at the cathedral there – to Emily Dickinson's poem, *Tell it slant* (see page 49) – that 'Christianity indirect' has a parabolic, testing quality that's priceless because it's Christ-like. It doesn't hector or bombard but – praise God – leaves you space to think things through for yourself. It's such a space that Emily Dickinson's poem sees as the essence of the journey into truth. I hope the reader will discern this in what follows.

Rather than organise the services thematically I've presented them in the order in which they were given chronologically. This has the advantage of allowing the reader to dip in an out. Anything that was read or sung by others appears in italics. On the rare occasions when readers notice, for instance, that the Lord's Prayer is not italicised – as in the Daily Service I broadcast from Washington following Barack Obama's Inauguration as US President – this indicates that there was no choir, hence I read the text alone. To enable the book to supply the reader with enough devotional material for a season like Lent or Eastertide, I've also included five BBC Radio 4 Sunday Worship services that I've scripted and presented over the same period. The typographical presentation is slightly different for these services. As they involved a number of voices I've indicated these throughout the texts as well as providing more indication of the music involved to help the reader. I dare to hope that the services may prove useful models for those who have to construct similar such short devotions, assemblies for school or college use or who would like to develop something new. As is proved by the large attendance of shoppers and commuters at the fifteen minute service that ends each day in Braunschweig Cathedral – with which Blackburn Cathedral, where I used to work, is twinned – there is plenty of scope for such short 'preached liturgies'.

For all his aphoristic insightfulness, John Tinsley could be very impenetrable for small boys! I knew there was something in the Dickinson poem he'd quoted and I loved its imagery but I also knew that I needed someone to translate for me. That someone – a very gifted broadcaster himself – was David Isitt, a canon residentiary at Bristol Cathedral – from whose Eastern Lady Chapel, incidentally, daily service was broadcast during two of the Second World War years, 1940 and 1941. David knew all about small boys and – as a very gifted classicist, too – he understood very well the need for translation. As a priest and pastor, it was what he did best.

Later he taught me that the art of preaching lay in becoming "more understandably enigmatic," which is the sort of phrase that – in his words again – "ought to tease the laziest of us into some kind of active thought."

I loved and respected David in a way I have loved few people in my life. I owe him – and his wife Verity – more than they can ever know and I can ever repay.

I can only hope that he would feel this book worthy of his memory and all he sought to teach me about telling it slant, and that Verity will accept it as a small thank you for years of kindness, friendship and support.

Acknowledgements

This book would not have been possible without the kindness and encouragement of many people. I owe a particular debt to everyone who's worked on the BBC Daily Service, the Act of Worship and Sunday Worship programmes with which I've been involved: producers, sound engineers, technical, broadcast and support assistants; singers, readers, organists and directors of music; and listeners who've been kind enough to email or write responses to many of the services. A master of the Daily Service genre, who is also a good friend – Leslie Griffiths – has very generously contributed a foreword.

The sermon preached at the service (46) from the Lambeth Conference is reproduced from the website (http://www.archbishopofcanterbury.org/1907) by kind permission of the 104th Archbishop of Canterbury. It remains copyright © Rowan Williams, 2008.

The hymn *I am the light* written for the same service by the Dean of Canterbury is reproduced by his kind permission. It remains copyright © Robert Willis, 2008.

The collects also used in the same service (and the one included in 17) which were written for the Lambeth Conference 2008 by Canon Andrew Clitherow are reproduced by his kind permission. They remain copyright © Andrew Clitherow, 2008.

The Prayers of the former Bishop of Winchester, John V Taylor (10 and 44) from *A Matter of Life and Death* (SCM Press, 1986) are reproduced by kind permission of his Estate. They remain copyright © The Estate of John V Taylor.

Readers interested in following up the history of the Daily Service are directed to bookfinder.com where they should be able to find copies of Lavinia Byrne's book, referenced above, and also a book published ten years earlier, *The Church of the Air: celebrating 60 years of BBC Radio's Daily Service* (1988).

I'm grateful to the Right Reverend Nicholas Reade, then Bishop of Blackburn for a period of sabbatical leave from my duties at Blackburn Cathedral whilst I was on the staff there and to my former colleagues at the cathedral who made it possible for me to work on several publications, including this one.

With immense generosity, Niki, Carl, Daniel and Thomas Loubser, and Nancy and Steve Gordon, welcomed the Chivers *en famille* into their homes in Cape Town from November 2009 to February 2010, offering beautiful places to work and to think, and wonderful, relaxing hospitality. With the blessing of Richard Mason, its founder, a good friend and fellow trustee, staff of the Kay Mason Foundation warmly welcomed me into an office space in the centre of Cape Town with inspiring views and company, whilst Anjum Anwar MBE, Janine Brown and Alison Feeney made sure things 'back home' were running smoothly. The book should have appeared in the summer of 2010 but moving from Blackburn to London to take up new responsibilities as Vicar of John Keble Church happily delayed the venture and enabled me to expand it. I am grateful to the churchwardens, Parochial Church Council and the congregation for their encouragement to complete it. Brian Gannon and Martin Stabrey of Pretext Publishing were as ever only a pleasure to work with. I am very grateful to our eldest son, Dominic Chivers, for providing such a striking cover photograph, and to our middle son, Gregory Chivers, for the photograph taken during a recent Act of Worship at Broadcasting House. To them, to their younger brother Jonathan and to my wife Mary I express my deep love and thanks for all their support and forbearance.

Shuaib Karriem handled the text meticulously. As an editor and prof-reader he could not be faulted or bettered. His comments were always both perceptive and insightful, sensitive and challenging. The significance of the writer-editor relationship was perhaps heightened in this case by the fact that Shuaib embraces a faith perspective different from my own. The Christian-Muslim conversations that resulted were in microcosm what telling it slant is meant to be about. In the process we were both I believe much enhanced and we became the best of friends. I am immensely grateful to him for all that he has contributed. Any mistakes that remain are mine alone.

London
January 2013

1. Holy is the Lord: Aaron

2 August 2006

Good morning.

Twice in my ministry as a priest, I've lived and worked in London and, like millions of others, had cause to travel by tube almost every day. I can't claim that sharing such a confined space during the rush hour was exactly my idea of fun. But as a dog-collar-wearing tube-user I certainly had some extraordinary conversations with people.

There was the woman with a love-life, the complexity of which would have taxed the script-writers of *Desperate housewives* – who wanted me to help her whittle down the number of her partners right there and then. I'd never thought of myself as a kind of ecclesiastical Cilla Black – it was all a bit much at 7:30 on a cold February morning. But the young lovers, on their return from Paris following a romantic weekend, who asked me to bless their relationship, the elderly man who'd recently buried his only son and who wanted a shoulder to cry on, as well as the drunken soul who simply held my hand because he believed that it would bring him more luck than he'd had on other days of late, all of these fellow tube-travellers left a deep impression.

Any packed tube is of course a microcosm of our society, its hopes, fears and confusions. And it's the job of every priest – indeed of every person of faith – to get struck into this melee, to listen to the stories that people tell and to share the joy and the pain that's on offer.

This week our theme is holiness, the holiness of the Lord as reflected through people. We tend to think of holiness as a churchy, or otherworldly thing. We call Basil Hume or Mother Teresa holy. But we don't tend to describe one another like that – except in a rather dismissive way, when we detect piety that's fake. But as I've discovered on the tube, there's plenty of holiness out there, if only we're attuned to it. And as the striking words of our first hymn O God of earth and altar suggest, such holiness can actually be the glue that holds a society together

Hymn: O God of earth and altar

O God of earth and altar, bind us together, we pray, that alive to your presence in the world we may celebrate your transforming holiness, wherever it is to be found. *Amen.*

The words of that first hymn by GK Chesterton are not exactly for the faint-hearted. They sound very harsh, judgmental even, in our contemporary context. But that's because they point to some uncomfortable truths about the three letter word which is the opposite of holiness, that little word 'sin' which some people seem to avoid nowadays as if one way or another you can bypass reality and become holy without sorting out your faults and failings. But much as we try to avoid the reality of our human sinfulness we have only, for instance, to put Chesterton's words into the context of the bomb craters and wrecked buildings of Israel and Lebanon, or the less obvious but no less discernible cracks and craters in our own relationships, we've only have to think of things from our perspective, let alone the global one, to realise that sticking our heads in the sand isn't much use when they're actually already in the fire!

But when, like the priest Aaron in our reading this morning, we notice the cracks and craters in human living, when like Aaron's son Eleazar we're prepared to take responsibility for your own faults and even for those of others, and make atonement for them, then we can experience the extraordinary and transforming holiness of God.

Reading: Numbers 16: 36-40, 46-48

Then the Lord spoke to Moses, saying: Tell Eleazar son of Aaron the priest to take the censers out of the blaze; then scatter the fire far and

12

wide. For the censers of these sinners have become holy at the cost of their lives. Make them into hammered plates as a covering for the altar, for they presented them before the Lord and they became holy. Thus they shall be a sign to the Israelites. So Eleazar the priest took the bronze censers that had been presented by those who were burned; and they were hammered out as a covering for the altar just as the Lord had said to him through Moses.

Moses said to Aaron, 'Take your censer, put fire on it from the altar and lay incense on it, and carry it quickly to the congregation and make atonement for them. For wrath has gone out from the Lord; the plague has begun.' So Aaron took it as Moses had ordered, and ran into the middle of the assembly, where the plague had already begun among the people. He put on the incense, and made atonement for the people. He stood between the dead and the living; and the plague was stopped.

Anyone who's ever travelled on the tube will doubtless be familiar with the voice from the heavens that instructs them to "mind the gap" as they leave the carriage. In terms of personal safety it's a sensible instruction to follow if you aren't to end up falling off the platform and onto the track.

But in terms of keeping ourselves spiritually on track we actually have to do the opposite – we need to step into the gaps of life rather than stepping over or avoiding them. As Aaron was called by Moses, so we're called by God to mind and to mend our own lives, and the lives of those around us. It may sound a bit daunting and sometimes – if we're really honest – unappealing too. It will mean chatting to strangers or letting them cry on our shoulders. But most often it will involve simply standing alongside them, not saying or doing anything in particular but just being there for them, waiting with them in their suffering or confusion or pain, for signs of a new dawn.

Choir: We wait for thy loving-kindness, O God, William McKie

Sir William McKie's anthem, We wait for thy living kindness, O God. So we wait on God in prayer.

We pray for the courage to step into the gaps we see in the world around us, and for the patience to wait with God in those gaps, as he uses us to reveal his compassion and love.

We remember all who step into the most difficult situations in our world: diplomats seeking to bring normality amidst the chaos of conflict, friends and family alleviating the pain of grief, or ensuring a safe space for children when relationships break down around them, care workers who inhabit the run-down spaces of our cities and towns to bring hope to drug-users, to the homeless, and to refugees.

As we pray for all who feel that they are falling through the cracks of life, we remember especially the child-victims of the on-going conflict in the Lebanon and in Israel, and all the bereaved.

God ever-merciful, whose Son our Saviour lived among us as the Prince of Peace: give us grace to be your peacemakers, to transform hatred by dialogue, conflict by patience and love, through the same Jesus Christ our Lord. *Amen.*

Our Father …

As we pray for peace in a time of uncertainty and violence so we ask that God will purify our motives and actions as we sing the song: *Restore, O Lord, the honour of your name!*

Song: Restore, O Lord, the honour of your name!

So may God restore in us the honour of his name, recreate for us a space within which to await new possibilities, and reaffirm through us his love for the whole world. And may the blessing of God Almighty, the Father, the Son and the Holy Spirit, be upon us this day and always. *Amen.*

2. Christmastide: St John the Evangelist

27 December 2006

Good morning.

After the festivities of Christmas and Boxing Days, the bright lights of seasonal sales will attract millions this morning, as they head off to the high street in search of the bargain that never quite made it into Santa's little sack.

Estimates vary as to how much money we spend both before and after Christmas, and whether we can really afford to do so. The consensus seems to be that we can't and that we're getting ourselves further and further into debt as a nation. Whatever the truth of that may be, what isn't in doubt is that those seductive bargain basement lights lead most of us pretty quickly – within a couple of days in fact – to avert our gaze from the light shining in darkness which has dawned in the babe of Bethlehem. So let's allow the choir to re-summon us to the stable as they sing John Joubert's carol, *Torches*.

Choir: Torches, John Joubert

Light of the world, as you lead us again to Bethlehem, be born in us, we pray, that we may transmit the warmth of your light and the transforming power of your love to those around us. *Amen.*

As an antidote to our perennial escape into consumerism, I've been trying, in the remaining days of his centenary year, to hold onto some wonderful words of John Betjeman. If I found a Betjeman book in every bargain basement I'd be a happy man since I love his distinctive combination of predictable rhythm and piercing insight.

'The time draws near the birth of Christ, a present that cannot be priced' he cautions to those who get too sucked into the commercialism of Christmas and its aftermath – 'the bath salts and inexpensive scent, the hideous tie so kindly meant' – as he puts it in another poem. We've all no doubt had or even, dare we admit it, given our fair share of those kinds of presents this Christmas.

Of course the present that matters most was, as Betjeman continues, 'given two thousand years ago. Because if God had not given so He still would be a distant stranger And not the Baby in the manger.'

There's a truth that just trots off the tongue. But what a thought: that without that baby we wouldn't in fact know very much about God at all. This is precisely the driving metaphor for the poet and evangelist John, whose life and wonderful writings the church celebrates today. Because the evangelist John's extraordinary claim is that into the basement of our world, life as it should be lived is shown to us in the neediness of a baby, in the light and life of God become a human being. Let's listen to the beautifully poetic way in which John puts this in his first letter.

Reading: 1 John 1: 1-7

We declare to you what was from the beginning, what we have heard, what we have seen with our eyes, what we have looked at and touched with our hands, concerning the word of life – this life was revealed, and we have seen it and testify to it, and declare to you the eternal life that was with the Father and was revealed to us – we declare to you what we have seen and heard so that you also may have fellowship with us; and truly our fellowship is with the Father and with his Son Jesus Christ. We are writing these things so that our joy may be complete.

This is the message we have heard from him and proclaim to you, that God is light and in him there is no darkness at all. If we say that we have fellowship with him while we are walking in darkness, we lie and do not do what is true; but if we walk in the light as he himself is in the light, we have fellowship with one another, and the blood of Jesus his Son cleanses us from all sin.

In the Christmas season we have a clear choice; we can chase any number of bargains we regretted not finding in our stocking when we awoke on Christmas morning. We can live the lie of that quest and keep up with the Jones's. We can follow the bright lights of illusory pleasures of all kinds. Or we can venture towards the present that cannot be priced which offers us genuine light and, in one of the evangelist John's most frequently-used words, life, aliveness. I came to bring you alive, to give you this kind of aliveness, switched-on-ness in all its abundance, says John's Christ.

And on the face of it, that seems to offer us an easy choice. But we all know that sadly it isn't that easy. There's something after all much more appealing about a bit of escapism into retail therapy rather than the reality of the nappy-changing demands to which we'll have to respond, if we really attend to the child in the manger. Babies are demanding: extraordinary gifts to us. But the infant Christ is unique: a special gift, the source of light and transformation for us all. Let's give thanks for this, as we hear the carol, A great and mighty wonder, to music by the seventeenth century composer Praetorius.

Choir: A great and mighty wonder, Michael Praetorius

The evangelist John gave as pictures of life and light that make a great impression. He put the truth of God incarnate into an unforgettable image, when he spoke of 'the Word made flesh'. That's an astonishing image, a mystery literally to take our breath away or to open our eyes in wonder. But it's a mystery that says something not just about God but about us. For as we gaze at a cot or a manger we realise that we are in fact looking at the word, the God made flesh in each one of us. For we are looking at the mirror in which we see our truest selves. With that truth in our minds and hearts, let us pray:

We pray for life's bargain hunters – real and metaphorical – that they may not be so distracted by the dazzling brightness that lights their way that they neglect the true light shining in the infant Christ.

We pray that amidst the junk shop of faiths and spiritualities, its confusions and tensions, seekers and pilgrims may always discover the pearl of greatest price, which is the gift of real life made known in God's love for every soul.

We pray for all who do not know this love, who cannot feel it or have become numbed to its liberating qualities. We pray for the sick and the lonely, for all who lack food or shelter, education or employment opportunity. May our concern ignite the light of hope in their lives.

So let us pray that the life of God's kingdom of light and love may come in all its fullness:

Our Father …

And so we pray for grace to recognise the light and love which dawns in Jesus Christ: Joy to the world! The Lord is come.

Hymn: Joy to the world! The Lord is come

So as God rules the world with truth and grace, the wonders of his love made known to us in our human nature, may the blessing of this same God, Father, Son and Holy Spirit, be upon each of us this day and evermore. *Amen.*

3. Loving God in action: the joy in doing God's will

18 January 2007

Good morning.

I've just returned from Boston, Massachusetts, in the USA, where I had the great privilege of attending a fantastic service during which a friend was ordained as an Anglican priest. The American Episcopal Church often gets a rough press these days, but my goodness they know how to do worship which blends the best of tradition and innovation, solemnity and informality in a way that's just so uplifting and inspiring.

For an Anglican like me with a love of the measured and the restrained, one who prefers the Holy Spirit's interventions to be planned and strategic, it was a bit of a surprise to say the least! The jewels on the mitre worn by Bishop Gail – a sort of African-American version of the Vicar of Dibley – were spectacular and never to be forgotten, as was the way she punctuated much of the service with 'Alleluya, brothers, Alleluya sisters, A-men.' The result was a feeling of absolute delight at the business of being a disciple, an amazing sense, as our theme puts it today, of the joy we are to feel in doing God's will: Sing alleluya forth ye saints on high.

Hymn: Sing alleluya forth ye saints on high

Christ our King, born to share our life, hopes and fears: fill us, we pray, with the joy of knowing your presence and doing your will, that the world may be transformed by the power of your love made active in us. *Amen.*

The contrast between the planned splendours or even the spontaneous joys for that matter of an ordination service, and a group of young Americans in their twenties with one older Brit huddled round a table playing Taboo, is pretty great. But this is how some of us relaxed – or 'hung out' as the Americans say – after the morning's liturgical marathon.

For those who don't know the game – it's often called Articulate this side of the pond – the object is to get people to guess the word you're describing without using the five words which have been identified as those most closely associated with it.

So if the word on the next card is *joy*, you won't be able to say smile, happiness, laughter, delight or elation. Enjoy playing Taboo as I certainly did I couldn't help sensing that a game where you don't get the clues that might most obviously tell you what's going on and what you're looking for is ironically quite like many people's experience of church. Since for much of the time – the Boston ordination aside – it does appear that Christians claim to be evoking joy in doing God's will when they worship, for instance, but without the telling signs that might indicate that this is in fact the case: the smiles, the happiness or laughter, the delight in one another that's not always, let's face it, that evident, let alone the elation that might be the result of all this worship.

This is odd, given that the quality Jesus most promised his disciples was a joy to draw them closer to one another and to make them whole; a joy about which we hear now in this morning's reading.

Reading: John 15: 7-11

If you abide in me, and my words abide in you, ask for whatever you wish and it will be done for you. My Father is glorified by this, that you bear much fruit and become my disciples. As the Father has loved me, so I have loved you; abide in my love. If you keep my commandments, you will abide in my love, just as I have kept my Father's commandments and abide in his love. I have said these things to you so that my joy may be in you, and that your joy may be complete.

When CS Lewis wrote his autobiography he famously entitled it, Surprised by Joy, a play on words, of course, since the name of the woman who surprised him with love, somewhat late in his life, was of course named Joy. But also a recognition that joy is often just so surprising. It's what we say that we crave as human beings, but it can sometimes be quite unexpected and somewhat overwhelming when we actually experience it.

When I was playing Taboo, I was overcome at times by side-splitting laughter. But what completely bowled me over was the reality that these people in their twenties, were not out clubbing or drinking on a Saturday night, like most of their contemporaries. No, they were actually saying to me that they were fed up with the illusory joys that many people chase week in and week out. What they wanted was quality time hanging out with one another: fun, fellowship and friendship.

But as I looked at their faces I suddenly realised that behind this quality, friendship time what they actually seeking was the deep joy, the wholeness, the truth they'd certainly discovered in one another and with which they were now surprising me. Because they were of course pointing me to the joy and truth of the one who saw life not as an endless quest for superficial pleasure – a quest that in reality pretty soon becomes a drudge or a dirge – no, the one for whom the journey through life was a dance, a dance we are all invited to join.

Choir: Lord of the Dance, Shaker tune, adapted Sydney Carter, arranged Stephen Jackson

That exuberant arrangement of the American Shaker tune, The Lord of the Dance, was by Stephen Jackson. It reminds us not only that we find ourselves or strengthen friendships amidst the dance of life, but that step by step we are being helped to discover the liberating joy of God's will, his special purpose for each one of us too, as he lives in us and we in him.

So we give thanks for the joy of God's presence as Lord of the dance, that where-ever we may be we'll allow God to lead us more deeply into the dance of life.

We express our gratitude for the abundant gifts which we receive each day: for food, fellowship and friendship; for the extraordinary joy of God's Spirit within us; that sharing these gifts with others our joy may be complete.

We pray for all at this time unable to feel joyful, for the sick and the suffering, the lonely and the bereaved; for the traumatised or the wounded, the battle-torn or the hungry; for all who feel resentful as a result of happiness which is near or far from them: may their pain or brokenness be made whole through our joy turned into compassion.

That our joy may be completed as we embrace God's kingdom, we pray in the words which Jesus gave us: *Our Father ...*

With a note of joy Jesus introduced the heart of his Gospel message, a message that can change everything for those who follow it: A new commandment I give unto you, that you love one another as I have loved you.

Hymn: A new commandment I give unto you

So as we seek to love one another and to share the joy of God with neighbour and stranger alike, may the blessing of this same God, Father, Son and Holy Spirit, be upon each of us this day and evermore. *Amen.*

4. Trial and execution (Holy Week): Trial before Pilate

4 April 2007

Good morning.

Imagine sitting in a room high above a great city, looking out on its bustling streets, crammed with tired and over-excited pilgrims gearing up for the year's biggest Festival. Imagine that you are the person responsible for keeping order in such a place, a city full of tiny back streets, with hawkers selling their wares and people up to no good. From your look-out, you suspect that all over the place there are tin-pot revolutionaries plotting away behind the shuttered windows of dark alleys. And then you hear the shouting begin, a solemn procession of people heading for the big religious venue, chanting for their Galilean leader Jesus, chanting, All glory laud and honour to the redeemer King.

Hymn: All glory laud and honour

Gracious King, who delights to receive the praises of your people, look with compassion on us as our acclamation turns to betrayal and rejection. Look on us, Lord, with your redeeming love. *Amen.*

Pontius Pilate, the man gazing with foreboding from that upper room in first century Jerusalem has not had a good press across Christian history. He was a kind of first-century Robert Mugabe, a twisted ruler who would do whatever it took to feed his addiction to high-living and power. Indeed, the openness with which Robert Mugabe has, in the past few days, tried to explain the recent beating of Morgan Tsvangirai, the Zimbabwean opposition leader, as if this could somehow logically be justified, all this closely parallels in historical terms the kind of man Pilate was: intelligent but heartless, able yet insecure to the point of delusion about himself let alone the man from Nazareth who appeared before him, whom he saw as just another Galilean trouble-maker.

Reading: John 18: 33-40

Then Pilate entered the headquarters again, summoned Jesus, and asked him, 'Are you the King of the Jews?' Jesus answered, 'Do you ask this on your own, or did others tell you about me?' Pilate replied, 'I am not a Jew, am I? Your own nation and the chief priests have handed you over to me. What have you done?' Jesus answered, 'My kingdom is not from this world. If my kingdom were from this world, my followers would be fighting to keep me from being handed over to the Jews. But as it is, my kingdom is not from here.' Pilate asked him, 'So you are a king?' Jesus answered, 'You say that I am a king. For this I was born, and for this I came into the world, to testify to the truth. Everyone who belongs to the truth listens to my voice.' Pilate asked him, 'What is truth?'

After he had said this, he went out to the Jews again and told them, 'I find no case against him. But you have a custom that I release someone for you at the Passover. Do you want me to release for you the King of the Jews?' They shouted in reply, 'Not this man, but Barabbas!' Now Barabbas was a robber.

Like all tyrants, Pilate took the coward's way out. He understood a little about Jesus but not enough. The product of this was a hasty decision simply to get rid of a man perceived to be a threat and alleged to be a self-proclaimed king. Of course, he wouldn't do the deed himself. He had, like Mr Mugabe, security police for that. Indeed, like the Zimbabwean president again, since he was no mean orator, he could go one better. Pontius Pilate, he knew how to get a crowd going and to swing them to his side in an instant. Let them take the blame if Jesus died and a real criminal was allowed back onto the streets. It wouldn't be his decision. It would be theirs.

But the story isn't of course just about Pilate. It's about Jesus too and the gently insistent, compassionately reflective way he reacts to his oppressor.

Recently, I found myself watching again that amazing film *Shooting dogs*, which tells the story of a priest living through the Rwandan Genocide. It's not a story that can easily be summarised. But at the film's end, when the priest has done his best to ensure the safety of the youngest members of his flock, he stands at a checkpoint facing, like Jesus before Pilate, a man who has the power to kill or to release him, a man who is literally pointing a gun straight at him. Like Jesus, he knows that this man will actually pull the trigger, and that his ministry will end in costly sacrifice. But seconds before the priest is shot we hear him say to his killer: "When I look into your eyes, all I see is love."

Pilate couldn't see the love which stared him in the face, the truth which, as the evangelist John says elsewhere, could actually set him free from all his insecurities, if only he'd bother to notice it. But all Pilate sees is a threat, a threat which his clouded mind turns into the face of an evil, a wickedness that must be stopped.

Choir: Psalm 140: Deliver me from the evil man, WE Smith

Those words of Psalm 140, sung to Anglican chant are of course two-edged. On the one hand they remind us how easy it is to see threats and enemies that simply aren't there. On the other, they represent the heart-felt plea of a suffering people.

So we pray for all who oppress others, who make a show of power which simply reveals their own desperate insecurity. We pray that we may never wash our hands of them, but challenge and confront them with the transforming power of love.

We pray for all who suffer at the hands of tyrannical leadership, remembering at this time of great pain for them, the people of Zimbabwe.

We pray that the poverty of our own sight and insight may be transformed through the richness of the love we see in Jesus and he sees in us.

We pray for all for whom life itself is a trial: for the sick and the suffering, the lonely and the unloved, the vulnerable and the abused.

We pray with the Christ who taught his disciples to ask that they may not be brought into temptation, may not come to the time of trial, as we say together: *Our Father ...*

As we stand this Holy Week alongside the Christ who faces Pilate so we praise this Christ who is King of kings, majesty, God of heaven living in me.

Song: King of kings, majesty

As we seek to look through the eyes of Love: eternal, faithful and true, may the blessing of this same God be upon each of us this day and evermore. *Amen.*

5. Christ triumphant (Ascensiontide): Promise of the eternal kingdom

24 May 2007

Good morning.

A few days ago a colleague of mine approached me saying that he thought I was looking a bit tired. 'Are you suffering from seasonal affective disorder,' he asked – SAD as the acronym runs. 'There's so little sunshine and so much grey sky and rain in Lancashire,' he joked, 'I wouldn't be surprised if all of us weren't suffering from it.' 'The only SAD I'm suffering from,' I quipped, 'is seasonal ascension disorder.' He looked puzzled. 'What on earth's that?' 'Earth,' I replied, 'doesn't have much to do with it … you get the disorder by listening to all those 'God is a space-rocket jetting to heaven' Ascension-tide sermons. A particularly bad bout comes when the preacher goes one stage further and makes a complete nonsense of the Ascension, informing you that Jesus had to go away so that the rest of us could get on with God's work.' 'What's the cure?' my colleague asked, 'The usual,' I answered, 'a decent hymn'… such as 'The head that once was crowned with thorns, is crowned with glory now'.

Hymn: The head that once was crowned with thorns

Lord Jesus Christ, King of earth and heaven, help us to be subject to your just and loving rule that we may begin to know the truth of your kingdom in this world and believe in the fullness of life before death as much as life after it. *Amen.*

Sermons on the Ascension often emphasise its spatial aspect: God going up. But that's a bit of a red herring. What matters is not

God going up but God being up, what we might call the divine ascendancy in the world, the Lordship of Christ, the power of his kingdom, as the Christian family prayer expresses it, experienced on earth as it is in heaven

It's a simple this-worldly much more than next-worldly message but that makes it a very demanding one of course, as our reading this morning makes clear, because we can't rely on some far-off heavenly realm where everything will be made better for us. We have, instead, to turn our hearts and minds to the painstaking business of living out the kingdom values right now, discerning the divine pattern or the golden string, as the poet William Blake puts it, which we are to wind into a ball across the length of our lives.

Reading: 2 Peter 1: 3-11

His divine power has given us everything needed for life and godliness, through the knowledge of him who called us by his own glory and goodness. Thus he has given us, through these things, his precious and very great promises, so that through them you may escape from the corruption that is in the world because of lust, and may become participants in the divine nature. For this very reason, you must make every effort to support your faith with goodness, and goodness with knowledge, and knowledge with self-control, and self-control with endurance, and endurance with godliness, and godliness with mutual affection, and mutual affection with love. For if these things are yours and are increasing among you, they keep you from being ineffective and unfruitful in the knowledge of our Lord Jesus Christ. For anyone who lacks these things is short-sighted and blind, and is forgetful of the cleansing of past sins. Therefore, brothers and sisters, be all the more eager to confirm your call and election, for if you do this, you will never stumble. For in this way, entry into the eternal kingdom of our Lord and Saviour Jesus Christ will be richly provided for you.

The promise is that somehow we'll be led to discover William Blake's golden string, the wonderful series of connections at the heart of that reading: faith producing goodness, knowledge, self-control, endurance, godliness, mutual affection and love, and that the result will, in Blake's words, 'lead us in at heaven's gate built in Jerusalem's wall.' But that's of course a thoroughly this-worldly not a next-worldly enterprise. It depends on how we see and show the ascendancy of the rule of Christ – the rule of love – in our lives now.

Today we're joined in our worship by the St George's Singers from Cape Town, South Africa, all citizens of a nation that knows more than most how to discover that golden string of love. Few societies of course have changed as much or as quickly: from apartheid pariah to democratic beacon. But that doesn't happen easily. To make heaven come to earth takes vision, an acute eye for the connections that need to be made.

And in the South African context I was powerfully reminded of this just the other day by a South African friend, Fr Harry Wiggett, the priest who ministered to Nelson Mandela during his long years in prison, both on Robben Island and at Pollsmoor on the mainland.

He tells many stories of Mandela but the best concerns the first time that Harry celebrated the Eucharist at Pollsmoor with a number of the political prisoners. The service was conducted under the watchful eye of the prison warder, Brandt, a rather typical apartheid functionary who sat next to the door. As the service was about to reach the Peace when all would share a handshake – a recognition of the kingdom in their midst – Nelson Mandela interrupted Harry, to shout across to Brandt: 'You're a Christian, Brandt, man, aren't you' 'Ja, meneer, yes, sir' came the reply. 'Well then, you mustn't sit at the door, you must join us over here,' which Brandt did.

Harry recalls this story with great humility since he hadn't thought to ensure Brandt's involvement. But Nelson Mandela included him, as he would include all South Africans in his vision of a new nation. And in that moment heaven broke through… a wonderful first step was taken in the rebuilding not just of one nation but of God's kingdom.

Choir: The Great Amen, Peter Klatzow

As the sound of that prayer-filled Amen siyakudumisa … Amen, praise the name of the Lord … rings in our hearts, so we pray with great thankfulness for the example of the Nelson Mandelas of our world who make connections that we so easily miss in order to show us the reality of heaven in our midst.

We give special thanks for the South African story of transformation, holding out to everyone the possibility of change, the hope that the kingdoms of this world may yet become the kingdom of our Lord and God.

We pray for all whose experience of life is far from hopeful, for those afflicted by the scourge of famine and pandemic, the threat of genocide, or the pain of conflict and war, especially in the Middle East. We remember all who are tempted to seek an end to life because their circumstances are intolerable.

We pray that by acknowledging the claim of Christ on our lives, we may be filled with his compassion and grace, to play our part in the strengthening of his kingdom.

We pray with the Christ who taught his disciples to do his will on earth as it is in heaven, saying together: *Our Father …*

We celebrate our call to discipleship as we acknowledge the divine light, love and power given to each of us to change the world: Siyahamb' ekukhanyeni 'kwenkhos: we are marching in the light of God.

Hymn: Siyahamb' ekukhanyeni 'kwenkhos / We are marching in the light of God

As we seek to live in the light, of God, may the blessing of this same God, Creator, Redeemer and Sanctifier, be upon each of us this day and evermore. *Amen.*

6. Psalms of hope and confidence: a psalm in time of despair

4 July 2007

Good morning.

The fantastic news that Alan Johnston, the BBC journalist in Gaza was released this morning by his kidnappers, reminds us that amidst despair there are always radiant signs of hope, hope from a God who leads us, as our first hymn acknowledges, o'er the world's tempestuous seas.

Hymn: Lead us heavenly father, lead us

Fill our hearts, O Lord, with the security of your unchanging peacefulness: calm our consciences, still our minds and transform our troubles through the power of your undying love. *Amen.*

I cannot imagine the range of emotions that Alan Johnston and his family must have experienced during his nearly four months in captivity. But, as he acknowledged in his first interview this morning, the fluctuation of feelings was considerable.

Even though he dreamt of liberation, whenever he awoke he felt completely hemmed in one room. When he spent twenty four hours chained up he really believed that he was going to die.

Yet, the gift of a radio also ensured that his spirits lifted and his heart surged when he realised the level of support for him right across the world.

That range of emotions is all there in the psalms, the book of the Bible that perhaps most expresses our experience of human living.

Listen to the psalmist as he feels hemmed in on every side and seeks to escape his captors, his enemies, fleeing from their clutches into the divine arms.

Reading: Psalm 55: 1-8, 22-23

Give ear to my prayer, OGod;
do not hide yourself from my supplication.
Attend to me, and answer me;
I am troubled in my complaint.
I am distraught by the noise of the enemy,
because of the clamour of the wicked.
For they bring trouble upon me,
and in anger they cherish enmity against me.

My heart is in anguish within me,
the terrors of death have fallen upon me.
Fear and trembling come upon me,
and horror overwhelms me.
And I say, 'O that I had wings like a dove!
I would fly away and be at rest;
truly, I would flee far away;
I would lodge in the wilderness;
I would hurry to find a shelter for myself
from the raging wind and tempest.'

Cast your burden on the Lord,
and he will sustain you;
he will never permit
the righteous to be moved.

But you, O God, will cast them down
into the lowest pit;
the bloodthirsty and treacherous
shall not live out half their days.
But I will trust in you.

Whenever I hear those words with their evocative image of the white dove lifting the psalmist from all the darkness that hems him in, I cannot help but recall the words of another Jewish writer who spoke to the world from the midst of despair.

This is how she saw things sixty years ago when dark clouds were engulfing our European continent:

"I see the world being slowly turned into wilderness. I hear the approaching thunder, that one day will destroy us too. And yet, when I look at the sky, I feel that everything will change for the better."

It wasn't a dove that provided the image of hope for this teen-aged writer, it was the sky.

"Whenever you feel lonely or sad," she wrote elsewhere, "try going to the loft on a beautiful day and looking at the sky. As long as you can look fearlessly at the sky, you'll know you're pure within."

As if that teenage girl actually had a choice to be anywhere else but the loft, the attic in which she gazed so often at the sky, and where her fearless words were found after she had been taken with her family from hiding to their place of extermination.

Ann Frank, whose diary was published exactly sixty years ago, was the psalmist for our times, re-establishing – amidst loneliness, despair and anguish – hope for a better world.

But is it really any better? We rightly delight in Alan Johnston's release earlier this morning. Yet as we hold on to this precious sign of hope we know that life within our own shores continues to be hedged about with anxiety at a terrorist threat we can neither be-lieve nor understand. Two steps forward, three back. It's a hard path indeed that we tread.

But as we hear now one of the most anguished cries in English music, Henry Purcell's setting of a verse from Psalm 102, Hear my prayer, O Lord, perhaps we will discern the truth God most wants us to grasp that amidst dissonance hints of resolution, of peace can always be felt.

Choir: Hear my prayer, O Lord, Henry Purcell

Let us pray

As we give thanks for the release of Alan Johnston, and for the many millions around the globe who have prayed and waited for this moment, we pray that God will use us all to be agents of peace.

Choir chant: The darkness is never darkness in your sight: the deepest night is clear as the daylight.

We pray that we may gaze fearlessly into the skies and by so doing sense the purity within ourselves which God wishes us to nurture, and to use as a force for good in our own communities.

Choir chant: The darkness is never darkness in your sight: the deepest night is clear as the daylight.

We pray for all who would destroy the fabric of our common life, especially those who would resort to acts of terror or violence, that they may embrace the best not the worst of their humanity.

Choir chant: The darkness is never darkness in your sight: the deepest night is clear as the daylight.

We name in our hearts those who continue to be unjustly imprisoned and all in despair this day, as in faith and hope that we may work for the creation of the better world we call God's kingdom, we say together: *Our Father ...*

As we celebrate the gift of freedom for Alan Johnston, the sign of a glory which always promises to transfigure despair, so on this American Independence Day we sing the hymn, Mine eyes have seen the glory.

Hymn: Mine eyes have seen the glory

As we walk with God seeking a better world may he change us from glory to glory and bless us with faith, hope and love, this day and evermore. *Amen.*

7. Mary, the mother of Jesus: understanding

14 August 2007

Good morning.

Are we there yet? It's not fair! His ice-cream was bigger than mine? You've guessed it: I'm just returning from the joys of a family holiday! A Cornish mixture of torrential rain and cloudless skies, cabin fever and challenging behaviour, laughter-filled lunches and lovely moments of thoughtfulness and kindness, all of which forces you to admit that for good and ill my family and other animals – in our case this included Harry the kitten and Hermione the hamster – is simply un-missable, if at times absolutely exhausting.

And it's of course that very mixture of the sublime and the caw blimee that God shared in an earthly home when as our first hymn reminds us he made the Virgin Mary mother of his only Son.

Hymn: Ye who own the faith of Jesus

Father God, we hold before you the joys and rewards, the tensions and challenges of family life: bless all families during this holiday season especially those with young children, that they may be places of love and exploration, security and growth. *Amen.*

One of the great things about holidaying in Cornwall is that it has something for everyone. I'm not a great beach person and in the flesh-fest I fair poorly. But that's fine because at St Ives, for example, whilst my children can romp around rock pools, my wife and I can usually box-and-cox parental duties so that we can retreat at some point to recharge our spiritual batteries. I usually head for the Tate or to an old favourite, the Barbara Hepworth

Sculpture Garden.

But this time, it was actually in the local parish church that I found some space. At first, it didn't look too promising as they were in the midst of a flower festival. But once I'd fought my way through the hyacinths and high heels – and that was just the line of venerable ladies patrolling the entrance – I reached the Lady Chapel, and the wonderful statue that Barbara Hepworth carved for it – of the Madonna and child – following the tragic death of her son when on active service for the RAF in Korea.

It's rather arts and crafts, Eric Gill-like in the lineage and lines of its beautiful Ocean-white stone. But it's most striking feature is the way in which as the child gazes towards his mother, she looks hauntingly not at him but beyond him towards the viewer. Was Hepworth, I wonder, trying to say something about loss, the isolation of mothers from their children in death – both from her own perspective and that of the Virgin Mary, as these two women experienced their respective Calvaries? Perhaps. But as I looked again I realised that the sculpture was actually speaking at a different level, saying something 'drectly', as the Cornish say, to me.

The haunting look was still a look of love, but love that understood the cost it must always pay if it's true. It was a look that certainly helped me to understand, as Mary so clearly understood in relation to Jesus, the role that I and my wife must play as parents walking the daily journey to independence with our children: their closeness and utter neediness on the one hand, their unique individuality and necessary separateness from us on the other.

All very much features of today's reading from the second chapter of Luke's Gospel.

Reading: Luke 2: 41-51

Now every year Jesus' parents went to Jerusalem for the festival of the Passover. And when he was twelve years old, they went up as usual for the festival. When the festival was ended and they started to return, the boy Jesus stayed behind in Jerusalem, but his parents did not know it. Assuming that he was in the group of travellers, they went a day's journey. Then they started to look for him among their relatives and friends. When they did not find him, they returned to Jerusalem to search for him. After three days they found him in the temple, sitting among the teachers, listening to them and asking them questions. And all who heard him were amazed at his understanding and his answers. When his parents saw him they were astonished; and his mother said to him, 'Child, why have you treated us like this? Look, your father and I have been searching for you in great anxiety.' He said to them, 'Why were you searching for me? Did you not know that I must be in my Father's house?' But they did not understand what he said to them. Then he went down with them and came to Nazareth, and was obedient to them. His mother treasured all these things in her heart.

In a wonderful poem, Walking away, Cecil Day Lewis takes his son Daniel to school and as he watches him run off with his friends without any goodbye feels somewhat slighted. It's a parting in fact that gnaws at the poet, but it also helps him to produce several of the best lines in English Literature as he realises through this experience what 'only God could perfectly show ... how selfhood begins with a walking away, and love is proved in the letting go.'

It takes great maturity to understand when to hold on and hold firm as a parent, or when to hold, even to bite your tongue and to let go. It's a degree of understanding I hope one day to acquire, not just in relation to my children, but also in relation to the rest of my family, my friends and even my faith. Which is where I find the figure of Mary so compelling because in her literally self-emptying life – the kind of life 'for others' into which each of us: mother, lover, friend and neighbour is called – she understands that love is indeed proved in the letting-go, in the spaciousness, the hard-won purity of a letting go which follows the pattern of the God who lets go of his Son to give us life itself. Blest are the pure in heart, the words of our anthem assert, to music by Malcolm Archer. Which means, blest indeed are those who have understood what it is to let go.

So as we pray that our hearts may be temples fit for God's dwelling place, we remember our homes and those closest to us. We pray that we may always provide them with the space within which to develop and thrive.

We pray for all children in situations of vulnerability, for parents who lose control or hope, for young people as they make the difficult and demanding transition into adulthood, that they may do so confident in their emerging identity and roots, receiving respect from those around them and returning this in equal measure.

We recall with horror the death of Garry Newlove beaten to death by a teenage gang in Warrington. As we pray for his wife and daughters we remember all those who express their identity through acts of mindless violence, that their lives may be transformed.

We remember on this, the sixtieth anniversary of Partition, those in Pakistan and India, and beyond, who continue to bear its scars that, seeking to let go of past enmity and bitterness, all may seek a shared future as God makes each of us his dwelling place. Amen.

So we pray that God will make us his dwelling place as we sing the hymn: Lord of the home.

Hymn: Lord of the home

May the presence of God sanctify our hearts and homes as places of welcome and grace, and make each duty we fulfil an offering of love, this day and evermore. *Amen.*

8. Envy and jealousy: Joseph and his brothers

4 September 2007

Good morning.

"My brother was the apple of Dad's eye. He could get away with anything. Dad spent so much time with him, he hardly noticed I existed."

Agnes – let's call her Agnes – was pouring her heart out to me. In her eighties, envy and jealousy filled her frail voice as she talked about her brother John; disdain, boiling over into anger as she referred to her father.

What was I to do to help Agnes unpack a lifetime's resentment about John, about her Dad, the world, almost everyone it seemed, onto whom she'd clearly been projecting this pain for so long?

The unforgiving heart that broods on wrongs, and will not let old bitterness depart. This was Agnes. It can no doubt so often be you or me as well. So let's pray this morning for grace to let go of our resentments as the choir sings the hymn: Forgive our sins as we forgive.

Hymn: Forgive our sins as we forgive

Lord, cleanse the depths within us where resentment and bitterness lurk. Help us to take the first steps on the road to reconciliation with those towards whom we harbour hatred. Instead, make of our anger and pain a well-spring of peace and love. *Amen.*

As a priest I spend a good deal of my time with individuals in pastoral conversation. That's what a priest's for. But if I was paid a tenner for each time I chatted to someone whose inner-being was being torn-apart by envy or jealousy I'd have retired a tax exile long ago!

Jealousy and envy. They're just two of the commonest root causes of dis-ease, physical, psychological and emotional. So it's no surprise to find them so frequently in scripture, whether it's the terrifying jealously of Cain that leads him to murder his brother Abel, the envy that sees Jacob disguise himself as his more hairy brother Esau – in a collusion with his mother that is both depressing and distressing – or the blockheaded stubbornness, bordering on stupidity, that sees some disciples in search of ring-side seats next to the Nazarene rabbi who's proving such a hit in first-century Galilee.

I wonder if anyone's counted the incidence of envy in the Bible? Someone must have done. It surely runs into thousands of examples. But the most famous example of all has to be the jealousy of Joseph's brothers towards their youngest sibling, the technicolour-coated shepherd-boy dreamer with ideas above his station and a father with eyes seemingly only for him.

Reading: Genesis 37: 3-11

Now Israel loved Joseph more than any other of his children, because he was the son of his old age; and he had made him a long robe with sleeves. But when his brothers saw that their father loved him more than all his brothers, they hated him, and could not speak peaceably to him.

Once Joseph had a dream, and when he told it to his brothers, they hated him even more. He said to them, 'Listen to this dream that I dreamed. There we were, binding sheaves in the field. Suddenly my sheaf rose and stood upright; then your sheaves gathered around it, and bowed down to my sheaf.' His brothers said to him, 'Are you indeed to reign over us? Are you indeed to have dominion over us?' So they hated him even more because of his dreams and his words.
He had another dream, and told it to his brothers, saying, 'Look, I have had another dream: the sun, the moon, and eleven stars were

bowing down to me.' But when he told it to his father and to his brothers, his father rebuked him, and said to him, 'What kind of dream is this that you have had? Shall we indeed come, I and your mother and your brothers, and bow to the ground before you?' So his brothers were jealous of him, but his father kept the matter in mind.

Envy and jealousy; so understandable, given that kind of scenario, predictable even. But are they inevitable? Only so, I believe, if we come at everything from our insecurities and succumb to one of our worst faults as human beings. This is what my family calls the 'me, me, me, I, I, I, self, self, self' complex: the inability to see life except as an answer to our own needs. But if we succumb to this disease, rather than overcoming it, envy and jealousy will soon be our bed-fellows because we shan't have begun to accept the unique gift from God which is our very self, let alone seen how we may contribute this not for our own gain but for the benefit of others.

There's an odd – and perhaps even paradoxical – truth tucked away here. Think about ourselves and we actually learn nothing about ourselves. Think about others – appreciate their gifts and talents – and we actually discover our own.

It's all a question of seeing and overcoming, lifting our lives above envy, falsehood and pride – as the words of our anthem put it – seeking instead to be lowly and humble, one who has learnt from others, from God.

Choir: Wonderful love, EL Wiseman arranged by John Bertalot

Wonderful love, takes us into our prayers:

Help us, O Lord, to prepare the ground of our being not for envy and jealousy but for mutual acceptance and love.

Choir chant: Seek first the kingdom of God: seek and you shall find

Teach us to do so by immersing ourselves in the gifts and talents of others, by encouraging and affirming, recognizing and relishing the uniqueness of each person.

Choir chant: Seek first the kingdom of God ...

Guide us to admit those ways in which we can be selfish rather than selfless, introspective and introverted rather than interested and engaged in friend, neighbour or stranger.

Choir chant: Seek first the kingdom of God ...

Make us to see the negative consequences of this in our personal relationships, as also its role in fuelling the conflicts which are such a feature of relationships between people and nations.

Choir chant: Seek first the kingdom of God ...

Give us grace to conquer all envy and jealousy through the humility of the kingdom for which we pray, in the words that Jesus taught us: *Our Father ...*

We close with a hymn which focuses our hearts and minds away from ourselves to God, as we pray that we may rise above 'jealousy, envy, rage and strife': 'Lift up your hearts!' We lift them to the Lord.

Hymn: 'Lift up your hearts!' We lift them to the Lord

As the trumpet call lifts our hearts above all that defaces and devalues our humanity, so may the Lord of love pour his blessings upon us this day and evermore. *Amen.*

9. Christ the Controversial: the Father's work

4 October 2007

Good morning.

"When you know what you're doing is right, this gives you the courage to go on doing it."

Those aren't my words; they're the words of James Mawdsley, the human rights activist imprisoned a few years ago for staging a pro-democracy protest in Myanmar (Burma) – words that he said to me one Good Friday when we found ourselves standing next to each other in the nave of Westminster Abbey, having a brief conversation.

As I've been praying, like so many others these past few days, for the Buddhist monks in Burma, I've thought a lot about those words of James's, because they take us to the heart of Jesus' life's work which our first hymn expresses so wonderfully as Immortal love, for ever full, for ever flowing free.

Hymn: Immortal love, for ever full

Controversial and challenging Christ, we hear your call amid the complexities of our times: give us the commitment to measure and test our lives by yours, and the courage always to pay the cost of true discipleship. *Amen.*

"When you know what you're doing is right, this gives you the courage to go on doing it."

But at what cost to yourself or your community?

All the Gospels offer an uncompromising answer to that question, an answer that can't be masked or hidden however much we try to domesticate the Christian message or lessen its demands.

Since they all attest that the cost that must be paid to fulfil God's wish that people enjoy life in all its fullness, is life itself. That's what it takes to make known the Father's love for the world. And as stones are again raised against Jesus in this morning's reading from John's Gospel we may be in no doubt about the cost to him or to those who are his disciples.

Reading: John 10: 31-36

The Jews took up stones again to throw at Jesus. He replied, 'I have shown you many good works from the Father. For which of these are you going to stone me?' The Jews answered, 'It is not for a good work that we are going to stone you, but for blasphemy, because you, though only a human being, are making yourself God.' Jesus answered, 'Is it not written in the law – "I said, you are gods"? If those to whom the word of God came were called "gods" – and the scripture cannot be annulled – can you say that the one whom the Father has sanctified and sent into the world is blaspheming because I said, "I am God's Son"?

In the end, people pick up stones to throw them at Jesus simply because of who he is.

But this isn't just a historical reality. It's happening right now. I recently heard the horrific story of a young man being beaten to within inches of his life simply for telling his family that he was gay; and another about a young woman stoned to death by her community because she revealed that she was HIV positive.

Who each of us is can seemingly at times be that threatening.

But it can also be utterly liberating and transforming.

When James Mawdsley was in a Burmese prison, facing a 25 year sentence, one of the guards seemed to be being particularly cruel to James. The man was clearly threatened by James's faith, by his dignity and his calmness. And as James watched him one afternoon, he realised why. For this guard knew at a deep level that he was in fact the one who was imprisoned, shackled by his functional place in the oppressive machinery of a state from whose clutches he might never be free. His cruelty came from his frustration. For he knew that though James was in chains, in heart and mind and spirit he would always be free.

And once James realised all this, once he could see that God's hand was on him, his feelings of hatred for the guard evaporated. Indeed, he went out of his way to be kind to his supposed captor, to lead him in the way that leads to all true freedom.

Choir: Lead me Lord, Samuel Sebastian Wesley

Words from the psalms set to music by Samuel Sebastian Wesley, for his anthem, Praise the Lord, O my soul, which take us into prayer.

Lead us Lord from despair to hope, from darkness to light.

Help us to recognise amid the controversies and complexities of life, that who each one of us is, is of infinite value to you.

Support and sustain us, that we may never be down-cast, even in the face of the most hideous oppression and violence.

Turn the minds and hearts of all who are threatened by their neighbours, for whatever reason.

Give each of us grace to pray for our sisters and brothers when they suffer the backlash, and are attacked for who they are, in Burma, in Zimbabwe or in Darfur.

And inspire us not only to pray for them, but also to work to set them free, as we embrace a vision of your kingdom and name you as 'Our Father.'

Choir: Our Father, Richard Stone

In an age which seems so often to have rejected or forgotten the reality of God's kingdom, we challenge ourselves to make God's love known, singing words by one of the winners of this year's Radio 2 Sunday Half Hour hymn-writing competition: words by Ellen Haining, set to music by Barry Rose, Where are the people?

Hymn: Where are the people?

So as we pledge to tell the world the reasons God loves us, the reasons he paid the ultimate price to give us life, may his blessing be upon us this day and evermore. *Amen.*

10. Altogether now (One World Week): Believing together

24 October 2007

Good Morning.

There's no shortage of believers these days; but those who feel a sense of belonging are few and far between. This was the conclusion that the sociologist, Grace Davie, reached about fifteen years ago in her book, Religion in Britain since 1945. Believing in God, thinking about the deepest questions in life is still what most people do, but they don't feel the need to belong to institutional religion – to be part of the church – in order to do so. But can you have one without the other from a mainstream Christian perspective? That's a big question about the nature of discipleship, but it's one we can't duck, as we sing our first hymn, When God almighty came to earth, with its insistent refrain: 'humbly follow me'.

Hymn: When God Almighty came to earth

Lord Jesus Christ, alive and at large in the world, help us to follow and find you there today, in the places where we work, spend money and make plans. Take us as the disciples of your kingdom, to see through your eyes and hear the questions you are asking, to welcome all others with your trust and truth, and to change the things that contradict God's love, by the power of the cross and the freedom of your Spirit. *Amen.*

John V Taylor

Often the answers to our deepest and most difficult questions emerge through prayer. And the prayer I've just used – words that John V Taylor, a former bishop of Winchester, wrote to ponder each day – give a direct answer to the dilemma posed by the phenomenon of believing without belonging. Is it possible to do one without the other? The prayer is emphatic: no, you have to do both, but notice that Bishop Taylor's words don't make the church – either as building or institution – the focus or even the context for believing, let alone for belonging. No, the prayer's focus is the world, the questions people are asking, our call to listen to these, to interpret and to understand them, to use them as a springboard for change, personal and communal.

What, you may be wondering, has happened to the Sunday services, the bring-and-buy sale, the Mothers' Union? To bishops, bible-study groups and synods?

"What's the definition of a synod?" a friend of mine asked me the other day. Answer: a group of people waiting to go home!

What's happened to all those things? They've been put in their proper place, in the perspective and the context God embraced and sanctified by coming to be alive and at large in Jesus Christ.

Reading: John 3: 16-21

God so loved the world that he gave his only Son, so that everyone who believes in him may not perish but may have eternal life.

Indeed, God did not send the Son into the world to condemn the world, but in order that the world might be saved through him. Those who believe in him are not condemned; but those who do not believe are condemned already, because they have not believed in the name of the only Son of God. And this is the judgement, that the light has come into the world, and people loved darkness rather than light because their deeds were evil. For all who do evil hate the light, and do not come to the light, so that their deeds may not be exposed. But those who do what is true come to the light, so that it may be clearly seen that their deeds have been done in God.

A few weeks ago I interviewed the outgoing Archbishop of Cape Town, the former Robben Island political prisoner Njongonjulu Ndungane, just prior to his retirement. He's well

known for his work to provide debt relief to the emerging econo-
mies of Africa, his attempts to combat the HIV/AIDS pandemic,
domestic violence and systemic poverty. These were all important
things, I readily acknowledged, but what, I asked him, was the
faith impetus to so much social action? Quick as a flash he came
back at me: John 3, where we learn not that God so loved the
church, but that God so loved the world that he sent his only Son
Jesus Christ.

And it's surely by believing together – as today's theme puts it
– that the world is actually the place where we are to locate our
sense of belonging that we'll realise the dream of togetherness at
the heart of this One World Week.

We may of course find something of that belonging in the
Church – for all our sakes let's hope so! – but let's be realistic; let's
express that hope with eyes open; since the experience for many of
the church right now is that it is pretty introspective and shut
down to say the least, inhabiting its own peculiar lah-lah land for
much of the time rather than the real world

Let's not then go for a discipleship that pins all its hopes on the
church. Let's instead set our store on the kind of believing which
reveals itself when we discover the many ways we belong to one
another simply as human beings.

But let's do so, with Jesus, alive and at large in the world, as our
model and guide, for as the old spiritual puts it, when we steal
away to Jesus, we discover, we embrace our ultimate belonging,
because we are finding our way home.

Choir: Steal away, arranged Michael Tippett

Michael Tippett's arrangement of the African-American spiritual, Steal away, takes us into our prayers.

We pray for grace to follow Jesus into the world today, to hear
the questions being asked there, as we show friend, neighbour and
stranger the trust and truth of divine love.

We pray for the courage and the imagination to see believing as the start not the end of a process that will finally embrace our deepest sense of identity and belonging.

We pray for the humility always to tread lightly when talking with others about God, realising that the divine imprint will already have marked their lives before ever we thought to identify his presence.

We pray for all those places where questions of believing and belonging have not brought togetherness but conflict or violence. We continue to pray especially for the peoples of Pakistan, Myanmar (Burma), Darfur and Zimbabwe.

We express our hope that we may know the peace and unity of God's kingdom as we say together: *Our Father ...*

Embracing the light, love and power of Christ we pray that he will lead us to the fullness of his kingdom, as we sing the South African traditional song, We are marching in the light of God.

Hymn: We are marching

So may we find the light, love and power of God alive and at large in the world today, and embrace them, as God makes of our lives a blessing for those around us, now and always. *Amen.*

11. Kings: Solomon

28 November 2007

Good morning.

This week we're thinking about kings and kingship, and our focus today is Solomon. We don't actually have a very clear picture of him in the Hebrew Bible, nothing like the impression of his father, David. And what we do have is not that complimentary. The First Book of Kings, for example, strongly suggests that he's simply a money-loving despot. Even his work to build the temple seems in truth to have been a by-product of a rather grand regeneration scheme for Jerusalem as much as an expression of faith and worship. But on the positive side he was renowned for his wisdom, hence the attribution to him of the books of Proverbs, the Song of Solomon, Ecclesiastes and the Wisdom of Solomon. All in all, like many kings, he was a bit of a mixed bag. But he did have this priceless gift of wisdom, the gift which our first hymn, God of grace and God of glory, suggests, when combined with courage, marks out a good king from the rest.

Hymn: God of grace and God of glory

Lord, grant to the rulers of this world wisdom and courage as they live out their days: that rich in the gifts of grace, all leaders may heal the world's warring madness and bring to glorious flower the bud which is the gift to us of your kingdom. *Amen.*

I've only twice in my life encountered kings. The first was the King of an African kingdom – with many wives – and his gift of a sacred cow that he wanted to walk up the aisle during a service at St George's Cathedral, Cape Town. I couldn't, I'm afraid, let him bring it, but that's a very long story. The only other occasion I've encountered kings, was when I met a clutch of them – if that's the right collective noun – all with their respective queen consorts, prince and princess offspring. It was on the morning of The Queen Mother's Funeral which I'd been helping to put together when I was a priest at Westminster Abbey.

Before the service, I was detailed with a colleague to keep an eye on what one television commentator – not from the BBC – called the 'holding bay' for visiting royals. It was in fact St George's Chapel just inside the Great West Door.

It's a small space and as so many crowned heads of Europe and their offspring gathered in it, so the noise level rose considerably with each arrival. Something had to be said, and there was no-one else to say it, so I gently got everyone's attention, and in characteristically diffident Anglican tones interjected: "I'm terribly sorry. I've no idea how I should address you all, but all of us will please have to try to chat more quietly." I said it with a twinkle in my eye which raised some smiles and even, on so solemn an occasion, a laugh or two. I guess I'll never be in such a position again. But as I walked away from the now much quieter group of Europe's crowned heads and their lines of succession, I realised that they'd been talking because on such an occasion, like any family facing the dauntingly public nature of a funeral, they were simply nervous. And that realisation made them of course just so much more human, ordinary, vulnerable like you and me; which in turn, made me reflect just how much we expect of our monarchs and leaders, living out their private emotional lives on so public a stage. As we learn, in our reading this morning, the expectations around Solomon were certainly very great indeed.

Reading: I Kings 3: 5, 7-12

At Gibeon the Lord appeared to Solomon in a dream by night; and God said, 'Ask what I should give you.' And Solomon said, 'You have made your servant king in place of my father David, although I am only a little child. And your servant is in the midst of the people whom you have chosen, a great people, so numerous they cannot be numbered or counted. Give your servant therefore an understanding mind to govern your people, able to discern between good and evil; for who can govern this your great people?'

It pleased the Lord that Solomon had asked this. God said to him, 'Because you have asked this, and have not asked for yourself long life or riches, or for the life of your enemies, but have asked for yourself understanding to discern what is right, I now do according to your word. Indeed I give you a wise and discerning mind; no one like you has been before you and no one like you shall arise after you.

For all the faults he later showed, Solomon seemed, as he started out as a monarch, to have an old head on young shoulders. He recognised the rich giftedness of the people he'd been chosen to lead and with whom God had chosen to make a covenant. He asked for the right things too and he got them: for an understanding mind and for the ability to discern between good and evil. So he intended that his kingship would be leadership exercised under the authority of the one who is our light and help, the stronghold of our life. It didn't exactly work out like that for Solomon of course, but it does for some monarchs, our own being one of them.

Choir: The Lord is my light and my salvation, David Haas

The Lord is my light and my salvation: words from psalm 27, reflecting the sovereignty of God, and taking us into our prayers:

We pray for all monarchs and for leaders everywhere. We give thanks for those, like our Sovereign Lady Queen Elizabeth, blessed with wisdom and insight, and we pray for all who lack these gifts, who are tempted to exercise power for its own ends, and at the expense of the welfare and well-being of others. We express our hope that they may acknowledge divine authority in all things.

Choir chant: With you, O Lord, is life in all its fullness and in your light we shall see true light, Taizé

We pray for our own sense of God's sovereignty, that he may reign in our hearts and use us to show forth his transforming grace in the world. We ask for the wisdom not to project onto our leaders unrealistic expectations or aspirations of behaviour or lifestyle we aren't prepared to embrace for ourselves. We express penitence for those ways in which we do project our own deepest fears onto our leaders.

Choir chant: With you, O Lord, is life in all its fullness ...

We pray for all places which desperately need to re-establish their sense of life lived under God: especially for the Holy Land, as Israeli and Palestinian leaders renew their commitment to walk the way of peace. We remember all in particular need, praying for Gillian Gibbons detained in Sudan that mercy may be shown to her.

We acknowledge the claim of God on us for in him is fullness of life, as we say the words of his kingdom prayer: *Our Father ...*

We express our hope that this kingdom rule will indeed be strengthened as we sing the hymn, Be thou my vision, O Lord of my heart.

Hymn: Be thou my vision

So may the King of heaven rule in our hearts and homes, and bless us with his vision of love and peace, this day and evermore. *Amen.*

12. From our fears and sins release us (Advent): a message of salvation

19 December 2007

Good morning.

"Have you brought a message of hope, Father?" This was the parishioner's question that greeted me when I arrived, one Sunday recently to preach at St George's Cathedral in Jerusalem. I was one of a group of peace ambassadors, together with Anjum Anwar, my Muslim colleague at Blackburn Cathedral, who'd gone to the Holy Land to support the latest Middle East Peace Initiative and to do so from an interfaith perspective. So I guess a message of hope or peace or something of the sort was expected. But I had to admit, much to the surprise of my questioner, that I hadn't brought the longed-for message of salvation to release people from their fears or sins, as our theme puts it this morning. "Why not?" he asked. "Well, I didn't need to," I replied. "It's here already."

Hymn: Angels from the realms of glory

Visit us, O Lord, we pray: pierce the gloom, scatter the darkness, and fill us with radiancy divine, as you call us to notice and to be embraced by the saving love you set before us. *Amen.*

"What d'you mean, you've found peace here already?"
My new friend at St George's, Jerusalem, was clearly puzzled by what, on the face of it, must have seemed a very strange assertion. Peace? In the Holy Land, of all places?

But yes, I'd discovered peace, the message of salvation, despite all the tension which saps the energy of so many and fuels the passion of others with a force that's often just so negative and destructive.

Yes, I'd seen peace in a Bereaved Families' Forum which brought together Israelis and Palestinians who'd lost loved ones in the conflict. A Jew whose teenaged daughter was killed when a suicide bomber blew up the bus on which she was travelling in down-town Jerusalem, now working with a Muslim whose brother died from injuries sustained in custody: both of them working together with community groups and politicians, in schools and in colleges to promote understanding, to model the possibility of co-existence and friendship, and to demonstrate that a measure of reconciliation is achievable.

I'd seen it, and heard it, in the free phone line they'd set up across the barrier so that though it's harder nowadays for Israelis and Palestinians to meet face to face, at least they can talk with one another. There've been millions of calls on those lines since they opened: not all nice calls of course. People expressing their hurt as much as their hope. But conversations, across a divide, that are happening and need to happen.

I'd seen it in Justin, a seventeen-year-old Canadian, who'd taken a year out of school to come to the Holy Land, to share life in a Palestinian refugee camp and to work with kindergarten children in Bethlehem.

Just as I'd seen it in the Haddassah Medical Centre in West Jerusalem, whose paediatric department gives free treatment to Palestinian children from East Jerusalem, using young Israeli soldiers doing their national service to spend hours providing educational and recreational support for these children.

For sure, it's a disjointed collage of peace amidst the ruins and remnants of ancient hatred and modern bitterness, but it's a collage nonetheless revealing the God of peace in people's midst. A God who, to the prophet Zephaniah, overcomes disaster and oppression, and transforms shame and conflict precisely so that the people of Jerusalem will have cause to be joyful.

Reading: Zephaniah 3: 14-20

Sing aloud, O daughter Zion; shout, O Israel! Rejoice and exult with all your heart, O daughter Jerusalem! The Lord has taken away the judgements against you,he has turned away your enemies. The king of Israel, the Lord, is in your midst; you shall fear disaster no more. On that day it shall be said to Jerusalem: Do not fear, O Zion; do not let your hands grow weak. The Lord, your God, is in your midst, a warrior who gives victory; he will rejoice over you with gladness, he will renew you in his love; he will exult over you with loud singing as on a day of festival.

I will remove disaster from you, so that you will not bear reproach for it. I will deal with all your oppressors at that time. And I will save the lame and gather the outcast, and I will change their shame into praise and renown in all the earth. At that time I will bring you home, at the time when I gather you; for I will make you renowned and praised among all the peoples of the earth, when I restore your fortunes before your eyes, says the Lord.

That ultimate restoration may seem some way off yet. But we know that it's possible. Look at Northern Ireland. No-one supposed in the forty years of my lifetime that Protestant and Catholic would be learning to live in peace with one another, let alone working actively together for peace. Peace may be more collage than jigsaw. We may not be quite sure how its pieces fit together. But wherever we detect one of them we are to proclaim its saving message and tell its transforming story. As I assured my questioner in St George's, Jerusalem, we don't necessarily have to bring peace from the outside – least of all in a colonial way! We just have to be able to spot it, and then to celebrate it. To let people know, as do the words of our anthem this morning, that despite all impressions to the contrary, Christ is still king over all the earth, because his reign breaks through wherever there is peace-making and wherever there are peacemakers.

Choir: O clap your hands, Orlando Gibbons

Music by Orlando Gibbons, setting words from Psalm 147, as a celebration of the Christ, the peace in our midst: words which take us into our prayers.

We pray for the people of the Holy Land: Christian, Druse, Jew and Muslim, Israeli and Palestinian. We give thanks for ongoing efforts to make peace across its many divisions. We praise God for the courage of the peacemakers he has set in the midst of such conflict.

We pray with and for all who are oppressed by fears for their security, by loss of movement, livelihood, land or loved ones. We pray for all who feel unable to communicate their concerns by any other means than resort to violence, that their hearts may be re-shaped as they hear the call to bring peace.

We pray for all who are weighed down or imprisoned by the painful realities of history, that their burden may be lightened through honest conversation and dialogue.

We pray for the wisdom and insight to notice the signs of peace that are there, to nurture, sustain and support them, so that light will indeed conquer darkness.

We pray for the coming of God's kingdom of peace in all its fullness as we say together: *Our Father ...*

Confident in hope that fear and sin, darkness and death, conflict and evil will always be defeated through the power of God's reign, our final hymn tells again of the message of angels proclaiming – 'Peace on the earth, good will to men, From heaven's all gracious King' – It came upon the midnight clear.

Hymn: It came upon the midnight clear

So may we send the song of peace that the angels sing into the whole world as God blesses our efforts as peace-makers now and always. *Amen.*

13. The path of holiness ... where prayer searches our hearts: developing a holy character

13 February 2008

Good morning.

A week is a long time in politics, so the old saying goes. But in the Church it can seem an absolute eternity! What a week we've had since the Archbishop of Canterbury's immensely nuanced lecture on the relationship of law and religious affiliation caused such levels of hysteria. Hostility, both from beyond the Church – and more depressingly from within it – which has done little to advance the debate or to recognise the innate holiness and prayerfulness of the man who tried to initiate it.

Today, in our Lenten journey we're thinking together about what it means to develop a holy character. We need models for this – and Archbishop Rowan Williams is surely one of them – but it all begins with the prayer which is the first line of our opening hymn: Teach me, O Lord, thy holy way.

Choir: Teach me, O Lord

Bless us, O Lord, in every task begun, continued and done for you. Fulfil your perfect work as you develop in us a desire to be made holy. *Amen.*

If anything proved that the Archbishop of Canterbury was right to invite a dialogue around the relationship between faith and secularism it's surely the unholy levels of rhetoric that have been heaped upon him in response. For a priest like myself, much of whose time is spent trying to foster relationships with the Muslim communities of Lancashire and beyond, it's pretty challenging to note increasing levels of Islamaphobia, the deep insecurities we seem to have as a nation about those whom we perceive as 'other', the sloganised character and sheer vehemence of the language with which we can speak to or about one another, not to mention the seeming inability of many to recognise the holiness of other faith traditions. Given all this, it seems that we're simply not prepared to have a conversation around issues which in the end are about the place of holiness not just at the centre of our faith but our society.

Which is where the call to holy living in today's reading from Peter's first epistle is surely so timely:

Reading: 1 Peter 1: 13-22

Therefore prepare your minds for action; discipline yourselves; set all your hope on the grace that Jesus Christ will bring you when he is revealed. Like obedient children, do not be conformed to the desires that you formerly had in ignorance. Instead, as he who called you is holy, be holy yourselves in all your conduct; for it is written, 'You shall be holy, for I am holy.'

If you invoke as Father the one who judges all people impartially according to their deeds, live in reverent fear during the time of your exile. You know that you were ransomed from the futile ways inherited from your ancestors, not with perishable things like silver or gold, but with the precious blood of Christ, like that of a lamb without defect or blemish. He was destined before the foundation of the world, but was revealed at the end of the ages for your sake. Through him you have come to trust in God, who raised him from the dead and gave him glory, so that your faith and hope are set on God.

Now that you have purified your souls by your obedience to the truth so that you have genuine mutual love, love one another deeply from the heart.

Do not be conformed to the desires that you formerly had in ignorance… instead, as he who called you is holy, be holy yourselves in all your conduct… love one another deeply from the heart.

In the Christian search for the truth of Jesus Christ in our own generation, try as we might, we cannot ignore those injunctions. If we use ill-judged language about those with whom we disagree, we aren't, in the end, very far on the journey to holiness. If we don't love those with whom we disagree … whether that's our fellow Christians or people of other faiths or for that matter secularists of every description, we clearly haven't made much headway when it comes to cultivating a holy character.

Which is where we need to let go of our own baggage, and to root ourselves in a life of prayer which begins, as do the words of our anthem, with one simple request: Lead me, Lord, lead me in thy righteousness, make thy way plain before my face.

Choir: Lead me, Lord, Samuel Sebastian Wesley

Samuel Sebastian Wesley's anthem, to words from the psalms which take us into prayer.

Lead us, Lord, from our tendency to fix the parameters of your agenda: take us towards an acceptance of the questions you pose for us in the life of our world.

Choir chant: Through our lives and by our prayers, your kingdom come, Taizé

Lead us, Lord, from our tendency to turn complexity into slogan: take us towards a deeper trust in your presence especially when we're confused.

Choir chant: Through our lives and by our prayers, your kingdom come.

Lead us, Lord, from our tendency to express our thoughts in too simplistic a way: take us towards a discovery of true simplicity of life.

Choir chant: Through our lives and by our prayers, your kingdom come.

Lead us, Lord from our obsession with self. Take us towards a recognition of those most in need at this time in Darfur, in Kenya and in Zimbabwe.

Choir chant: Through our lives and by our prayers, your kingdom come.

Loving God, you have called us into the life-giving way of discipleship. Lead us to be thankful for the privileges and challenges of this calling. Make us holy, Lord. Bring us to wholeness of life, for Jesus Christ's sake. Amen.

So lead us, Lord to embrace your kingdom of holiness as we say together: *Our Father ...*

Renew us in holiness and love as we sing: O for a heart to praise my God.

Hymn: O for a heart to praise my God

Impart your holiness, O Lord. Write your name on our hearts, as you bless us with your love, this and every day. *Amen.*

14. The contemplative path ... where we meet God: a glimpse of glory

10 March 2008

Good morning.

We've got to that part of Lent called Passiontide where the clouds gather around Jesus and his disciples, and things start to get very murky indeed. The frustration Judas harbours about Jesus' leadership style – which isn't to him anything like 'cutting edge' enough – is about to spin out of control. Darkness is descending. This is why our theme – a glimpse of glory – is so important. It's an antidote, something to hold onto, a sign. 'Show us your glory, O Lord', the words of our first hymn pray. That must have been the prayer of millions down the ages, the prayer of millions in the dark corners of our world right now.

Hymn: Yahweh, Ancient One, yet you're here today.

Show us your glory, O Lord. Let your goodness pass before us, right before our eyes, and we will call you Lord. *Amen.*

But what if God doesn't? What if we don't see his glory? What if it doesn't seem to pass by our eyes? Do we stop believing?

'I need a sign', a character says in one of the Monty Python films. That's a sign on a big scale. But we don't always get one, so what then?

These and other similar questions take us to the heart of faith and doubt.

I've always been encouraged by that wise saying of, I think it was Fr Kelly – one of the Kelham fathers – to the effect that the opposite of faith is not doubt but certainty.

Certainly, in my life, the grand signs have eluded me. They haven't passed in front of my eyes. But I've had so many little sideways-on or back-end glimpses of truth, that I begin to think they form a kind of piece by piece jigsaw that I'm nowhere near completing – I've just got a few bits round the frame's edges – but which is plenty enough, nonetheless, to be going on with. Perhaps it's only the back-end of truth that most of us glimpse.

That was certainly true for Moses, as we'll hear now in our reading from Exodus 33.

Reading: Exodus 33: 18-23

Moses said, 'Show me your glory, I pray.' And God said, 'I will make all my goodness pass before you, and will proclaim before you the name, "The Lord"; and I will be gracious to whom I will be gracious, and will show mercy on whom I will show mercy. But', he said, 'you cannot see my face; for no one shall see me and live.' And the Lord continued, 'See, there is a place by me where you shall stand on the rock; and while my glory passes by I will put you in a cleft of the rock, and I will cover you with my hand until I have passed by; then I will take away my hand, and you shall see my back; but my face shall not be seen.'

I remember from my childhood a wonderful sermon on that passage, which more accurately translated its concluding image as seeing the 'back-side' of God. It was given by John Tinsley, a scholar-bishop who had a sense of humour and really understood the enigmatic nature of the divine presence in the world: the way God speaks in parables and riddles, for instance, always avoiding 'Christianity direct' and the half-truth of religious slogan, even when he speaks to us through his Son Jesus Christ.

It was in that sermon that I first heard a poem by the wonderfully enigmatic American poet, Emily Dickinson, that's helped me to value this sideways-on, back-view God, of whom I catch such fleeting glimpses of glory.

Tell all the truth – Dickinson says,
But tell it slant
Success in circuit lies.
Too bright for our infirm delight
The truth's superb surprise
As lightning to the children eased
With explanation kind
The truth must dazzle gradually
Or every man be blind –

How right Dickinson is, since the truth of God would overwhelm us, blind us if we saw the full extent of his power and glory. We need, instead, as we're invited in our anthem, Power and glory, to come to the waters and be born again, but always recognising that it's a long labour, this journey to the fullness of light:

Choir: The power and the glory, Joyce Eilers

The power and the glory, with music by Joyce Eilers, and taking us into our prayers.

For the glimpses of glory we see in friend and stranger: in the touch of a hand, the reassurance of a smile and the tearfulness that results from our broken living.

We give you thanks, O God.

For the glimpses of glory we see amidst the complexities and confusions of life, the issues we cannot seem to resolve, the questions that just won't go away.

We give you thanks, O God.

For the glimpses of glory we must take on trust because they have been entrusted to others that we might believe.

We give you thanks, O God.

For the unique glimpses of glory and the rays of redeeming light waiting to be discovered in places of conflict and division, pain and suffering, darkness and despair, especially this morning when livelihoods, homes and whole communities are endangered by the storms and torrential weather in Wales and the South West.

We give you thanks, O God.

Teach us, O God, to see your power and glory made perfect in and through our weakness. Help us to glimpse it daily as you encourage us to pray for your kingdom, in the words that Jesus taught us: *Our Father …*

So we ask for grace to catch glimpses of divine glory in the world as we give praise to the Lord, the Almighty, the King of creation.

Hymn: Praise to the Lord

Creator God, let the Amen sound from your people everywhere, as you bless us with your glory this day and evermore. *Amen.*

15. Rejoice: gratitude

24 April 2008

Good morning.

'If you only say one prayer in your life: say thank you.' So said that wisest of all saints, Augustine of Hippo. To which his fellow African of a contemporary generation, the ebullient Desmond Tutu, once added: 'Start each morning by sitting at your desk thinking of all the people from the previous day you need to thank. Make their day by sending them a postcard' – I guess nowadays he'd say, send an email.

So let's think about who we must thank today as we listen to the hymn, Rejoice the Lord is King.

Hymn: Rejoice the Lord is King

Ruler of earth and heaven, Almighty Lord and King, as we rejoice in the gift of a new day, make our hearts so full with gratitude that no blessing will go unnoticed or un-thanked. *Amen.*

I don't know about you, but my mind's a bit too hazy most mornings to be full of thankfulness.

I'd like to say of course that this was because our one year old son had given us another sleepless night. But as I tend to sleep through his nocturnal calls for attention, I'd have to admit that my wife really has much more cause to feel hazy than me. Perhaps I'm just not the morning person I'd like to think I once was!

But whatever the reason, I seem so full of half-remembered chores, trivial worries and consuming concerns that as I sit at my desk I can't always get the focus I need to think-through my thank yous.

Of course, some of them are obvious – like the lovely meal someone gave me, which cost so much in terms of preparation –

but beyond this, who was that person who said something that made me think and later got me to change my views but whose thoughtfulness I didn't really react to at the time?

There was a spectacular instance of this the other day from a sixth-former who attended a lecture on technology and faith at Blackburn Cathedral where I work. It took the form of a question. "Which was the greater evil in the twentieth century," he asked, "technology or ideology?"

I'm so grateful to him for that searching question. I've now lived with it for days. I wish I'd made the effort to remember the name of the young man who asked it so that I could thank him.

I wish too that Horace Dammers – who was Dean of Bristol when I was a chorister there – was still alive to be thanked for all that he taught me. A copy of some meditations he'd written shortly before his death on Handel's Messiah dropped through my letter box and distracted me for hours the other morning when I was meant to be in a meeting.

They also made me remember a biblical technique for structuring my thank yous that Horace in fact taught me. It came from Philippians, chapter 4.

Reading: Philippians 4: 4-8

Rejoice in the Lord always; again I will say, Rejoice. Let your gentleness be known to everyone. The Lord is near. Do not worry about anything, but in everything by prayer and supplication with thanksgiving let your requests be made known to God. And the peace of God, which surpasses all understanding, will guard your hearts and your minds in Christ Jesus. Finally, beloved, whatever is true, whatever is honourable, whatever is just, whatever is pure, whatever is pleasing, whatever is commendable, if there is any excellence and if there is anything worthy of praise, think about these things.

Rejoice in the Lord, Horace would say. Always thank God first. Remind yourself next, not to worry about the day ahead. But if you've actually got some nagging worries get them out of the way so that they don't get in the way of your thank yous. Then, think on these things: who in the context of our relationships has recently been truthful when perhaps we didn't want to hear that truth? Who's been honourable when our thoughts or motives may have been less than honourable? Who's acted with justice in the face of our injustice and purity when we've perhaps somehow been compromising ourselves?

We know it works. We can try it now as we listen to the Choir of Royal Holloway College, London sing a sixteenth century setting of Philippians 4.

Choir: Rejoice in the Lord always, Mulliner Book

As we pray that the peace of God will keep our hearts and minds in Christ Jesus, we offer thanks for the questions which make us think, the insights which challenge and enliven us, the people to whom we owe so much.

Choir chant: Through our lives and by our prayers, your kingdom come

We give thanks for the God who inspires all that is commendable and worthy of praise: from the cheerful 'Good morning' that lifts our spirits to the act of compassion that stirs our soul.

Choir chant: Through our lives and by our prayers ...

We offer prayers for all who feel alienated by glib talk of a joyfulness they don't feel, for those whose pain, suffering or anguish makes thankfulness seem but a distant hope. We express gratitude too for those who support them in their darkness.

Choir chant: Through our lives and by our prayers ...

We give thanks for all who seek to turn sorrowful individuals into communities of rejoicing – in Zimbabwe, Darfur, the Holy

Land and in the back streets of our towns and cities.

Choir chant: Through our lives and by our prayers ...

We recall our own part in this work as we say the prayer that Jesus taught us: *Our Father ...*

We rejoice in the God for the fulness of whose kingdom we work each day, as the choir sings, Now thank we all our God.

Hymn: Now thank we all our God

All praise and thanks be given to the God, Father, Son and Holy Spirit whom earth and heaven adore, who guides us when we're perplexed and who blesses us on our way, now and ever-more. *Amen.*

16. The changing scenes of life: the future

19 June 2008

Good morning.

'I never think of the future, it comes soon enough.' So said that most perceptive of twentieth-century minds, Albert Einstein. But the truth is that it doesn't appear to come soon enough for many of us, judging by the amount of time we spend talking about our future plans.

How many of us, for instance, while away the odd hour thinking how we'd spend those lottery millions if we actually had the winning ticket: the holidays, the cars, the hotels, the meals: what fun it would be. But as my wife says, your chances of winning are only marginally improved by actually buying a ticket. Winning isn't likely, and there's an implicit distinction in all this between present and future, now and not yet. But it doesn't quite capture the Christian take on things, which is brilliantly encapsulated in the opening line of our first hymn, Now is eternal life.

Hymn: Now is eternal life

Bring to birth in us, O Lord, the new life which transforms our hope for the future into present reality. Reign within our hearts, and enfold us in the loving power of your resurrection, now and through all eternity. *Amen.*

I once asked Canon John Sweet, the distinguished Cambridge theologian to preach for me, and I've always remembered the way in which he described the Christian theology of time and eternity. 'It's as if we were living,' he said, 'between D-Day and VE Day. God's declared that victory's landed, on the beaches of Normandy – that's the movement of cross to resurrection. Victory's promised

71

for all. That's certain. What we need to do is to live in the light of that coming reality, in the light of VE Day which will see everyone sharing in the power of the resurrection.'

I'm paraphrasing from memory and something perhaps gets lost along the way. But the idea's an excellent way to describe the implicit tension between the fact that 'now is eternal life' and yet the fullness of all this still lies ahead. The charity, Christian Aid, came up with another way to encapsulate this in their slogan: we believe, they said, in life before death, a counter to the way in which some Christians can be too focussed on the hereafter to deal with the sufferings that too many experience right now. But, my goodness me, how difficult it is in fact to live today in the light of the resurrection, whilst also waiting for the fullness of the kingdom to dawn.

Let's listen to the advice which the Letter to Titus gives in this regard, in its second chapter.

Reading: Titus 2: 11-15

For the grace of God has appeared, bringing salvation to all, training us to renounce impiety and worldly passions, and in the present age to live lives that are self-controlled, upright, and godly, while we wait for the blessed hope and the manifestation of the glory of our great God and Saviour, Jesus Christ. He it is who gave himself for us that he might redeem us from all iniquity and purify for himself a people of his own who are zealous for good deeds.

Living in between worlds. Knowing we've had D-Day but with VE Day seeming a little farther off than it was in 1945, is very hard. But the secret, as the author of the letter to Titus suggests, lies in the quality of our waiting, a waiting we are to fill with that most urgent of human tasks, the task of the purification of ourselves and of our world. Purification. It's not a word we use much these days. But its suggestion of hearts and lives refined, tested, reshaped according to God's way points us to the heart of discipleship, which isn't of course about how little we have to do to qualify for salvation. It's about how much we must do to re-orientate ourselves in order to become channels of new life for the wider community. This can involve a lot of unlearning of those bad habits of thoughtlessness or selfishness into the grimy grooves of which we can too often get very stuck. It can also involve a lot of relearning of those truths about neighbourliness and kindliness that we only half-listened to all those years ago. Above all, it means embracing, taking seriously the commandments to love God and neighbour and ourselves: focussing on Christ and his sufficiency as way, truth and life, for in his example of self-giving love lies the key, of course, to everything.

Choir: Thou art the way, Christopher Steel

Christopher Steel's setting of Bishop Doane's poem, Thou art the way, which takes us into our prayers.

We pray for all who are imprisoned by false hopes for the future, for those who escape into a mythical future in order to avoid the harsh and painful realities of the present.

We ask for wisdom to stick with reality however difficult this may be, for patience and bravery to live in the now of eternal life, with all its risks and possibilities.

We remember all places where the now of eternity seems to be never-ending conflict, bitterness, tension and war, praying especially at this time for the people of Zimbabwe.

We pray for communities where life after death seems preferable to life before it because there is little food or drink, scarce material resource and little likelihood of change, remembering the relief effort now in Ethiopia, and reconstruction work continuing in Myanmar (Burma) and China.

We pray for courage to bring resurrection to such trouble-spots through advocacy for the down-trodden, compassion and prayer that is living and heart-felt.

O God, the protector of all who trust in you, without whom nothing is strong, nothing is holy: increase and multiply upon us your mercy; that with you as our ruler and guide we may so pass through things temporal that we lose not our hold on things eternal; grant this, heavenly Father, for our Lord Jesus Christ's sake, who is alive and reigns with you, in the unity of the Holy Spirit, one God, now and for ever. *Amen.*

Common Worship (Trinity IV)

So we pray for a daily share in the realities of God's kingdom as we say together: *Our Father ...*

As we look to the future and to the next steps we must take on our journey, we recall God's abiding presence with us and in us: Lord for the years your love has kept and guided, we bring our thanks today.

Hymn: Lord, for the years

Go forth into the world in peace; be of good courage; hold fast to that which is good; render to no one evil for evil; strengthen the fainthearted; support the weak; help the afflicted; honour all people; love and serve the Lord, rejoicing in the power of the Holy Spirit; and the blessing of God Almighty, the Father, the Son and the Holy Spirit be with us now and always. *Amen.*

17. Lambeth Conference: I am, be not afraid

23 July 2008

Good morning.

I've no idea what it must mean to wake up in the morning in fear of my life. But, here on the campus at the University of Kent, where the Lambeth Conference of bishops from around the Anglican Communion is meeting, and where I'm one of the worship co-ordinators, I'm surrounded by people who do.

Members of the Melanesian Brotherhood, a religious order from the Solomon Islands – who are at the heart of the Conference's Chaplaincy team – remind me that five years ago seven of their number were tortured and murdered trying to bring peace amidst civil strife. One of them had gone to meet a rebel leader to try and persuade him to surrender his weapons. When he didn't come back as expected, six of his brothers went in search of him. None of them returned.

I cannot imagine the fear they must have felt when they were held captive wondering not if but when their lives would end.

Most of us will never have to deal with that kind of fear. But some do. Let's think of them, and the tempestuousness that surrounds them as we hear our first hymn, Lead us heavenly Father.

Hymn: Lead us heavenly Father

Right now, tempestuousness doesn't come close to describing what is going on in Zimbabwe, a country haunted and hounded by fear. We can only hope that the decision to enter into some kind of power sharing between Robert Mugabe and Morgan Tsvangirai will in fact bear fruit. Sebastian Bakare, is right in the firing line of what is going on, as Bishop of the capital city, Harare. We hear something of his powerful story now.

The story of the life of the Church in Zimbabwe is not a very nice one but I think it is a story that needs to be shared. Since November, we have been denied access to go into our churches, and that has made a lot of people very angry, and I don't know how they are going to remove this anger. Because religion means a lot to our people. But to be told not to worship in a church you built yourself. You see a police officer standing there with a gun pointing at you saying you are not coming near. It's not a very nice experience. We live in fear. People have been killed. People have disappeared. People have had their hands chopped off. Some have lost their homestead. Everything that threatens life has been experienced by our people. So fear has been part of our life. But I think the disciples were so much comforted when Jesus said 'I am, don't be afraid'. I think people in Zimbabwe have been strengthened by their faith. There's no need to fear. I think I believe that if God wants me to be where I am he will protect me. Whatever happens I think I give my life to God. He is my creator, he will redeem me. Wherever I suffer he suffers with me. I'm not alone. But what encourages me most – why I don't have to have any feeling of fear – it is the support of the Anglican Communion. Wherever I've been on this campus people say to me 'We are with you'. That kind of solidarity has taken away my fear.

Taizé chant: Laudate tube

The courage of Sebastian Bakare and his compatriots is extraordinary and inspiring. But for most of us fear operates at a different level. Here, at the Lambeth Conference, there is inevitably quite a lot of it about the place. Fear that's developed on all sides of the Church over the last few years, because so often people have imputed motives and views to 'others' – that catch-all group which changes people from human beings with feelings and emotions, into card-board cut-outs with stances and views. A group onto which we may simply project our own fears. This is why the work of the Conference has been designed to move people beyond fear – through bible study on the 'I am' sayings of John's Gospel in groups of eight bishops, and larger groups of forty bishops meeting in a session called an indaba, which is a Zulu word for a village meeting where everyone speaks, listens and seeks consensus. As Ian Ernest, the Archbishop of the Indian Ocean, reminds us – reading words from John Chapter 6 – this is exactly what Jesus did when a storm blew up for his disciples and he came to them saying 'It is I' – the Greek can be translated, 'I am' – 'do not be afraid'.

Reading: John 6: 15-24

When Jesus realized that they were about to come and take him by force to make him king, he withdrew again to the mountain by himself. When evening came, his disciples went down to the lake, got into a boat, and started across the lake to Capernaum. It was now dark, and Jesus had not yet come to them. The lake became rough because a strong wind was blowing. When they had rowed about three or four miles, they saw Jesus walking on the lake and coming near the boat, and they were terrified. But he said to them, 'It is I; do not be afraid.'

Then they wanted to take him into the boat, and immediately the boat reached the land towards which they were going.

The next day the crowd that had stayed on the other side of the lake saw that there had been only one boat there. They also saw that Jesus had not got into the boat with his disciples, but that his disciples had gone away alone. Then some boats from Tiberias came near the place where they had eaten the bread after the Lord had given thanks. So when the crowd saw that neither Jesus nor his disciples were there, they themselves got into the boats and went to Capernaum looking for Jesus.

Music: from Peter Grimes, Benjamin Britten

That storm music from Benjamin Britten's opera, Peter Grimes, takes us into our prayers.

As bishops from around the Anglican Communion face the storminess of issues and concerns, we pray that the still small voice which says, do not be afraid, will be heard.

As each of us faces our tendency to dislike in others what we most fear in ourselves, we pray for honesty and integrity, for a spirit of self-criticism that may turn fear into hope.

As we hold before God the many around the globe who are fearful in our world, we pray that they may be cradled in the palms of God's hands, for each is known to God by name.

Using one of the special prayers written for the Conference, Archbishop Ian Ernest prays for the qualities each of us needs to overcome our fears:

Lord God, who came to the disciples by night
and brought them to safety,
we thank you that you have called us to lead others
through hazardous times:
grant us strength and gentleness,
wisdom and grace,
that in the company of Christ
we may uphold the tradition of faith we have inherited
and amidst the darkness of our present age,
may celebrate that communion of mutual understanding
and respect which you have called us to share with others.
Amen.

Andrew Clitherow

As we seek communion with one another and the whole of creation we say the prayer that Jesus taught us: *Our Father ...*

So we turn our fears and hopes into thanksgiving, recalling the promise of Christ to be with us, as we listen to the hymn, The Lord's my shepherd.

Hymn: The Lord's my shepherd

May the God who cleanses our consciences, heals our hurts, calms our concerns and stills our hearts, bless us and keep us this day and evermore. Amen.

18. Harvest praises: praise God from whom all blessings flow

22 September 2008

Good morning.

It's Harvest time, when churches echo to the strain of hymns whose focus is the wavy golden corn. Not that there's much chance, of course, for the corn to wave in Lancashire where I live. We've had so much rain this year that the corn's practically horizontal and some harvests have been ruined altogether. The other day when our eighteen month old, whose now busy learning to talk, briefly glimpsed the sun peeking through the grey skies above he jabbed a finger towards it, shouting, 'What's that?' What, indeed!

But if the sun's been pretty absent of late and the harvesting's been tough for some – and certainly it has this year – all the more reason to thank God for the fruits his creation has still so bountifully yielded, and to take up the theme of our opening hymn: Praise and thanksgiving, Father, we offer, for all things living you have made good.

Hymn: Praise and thanksgiving

Bless, O Lord, each person confessing your hand and your love in all things: speak to us through your creation and challenge us to share its resources for the good of all your children. *Amen.*

Always begin every day by thanking God for life's good things. That was the common sense mantra drummed into me each week at Sunday school. But it's easy to end up turning thanks to God for life's good things merely into appreciation for simply the good things themselves. I guess that's what consumerism is all about: an ever-expanding world of things to choose from and to own. A world believing that it can expand indefinitely – make a bid for eternity, if you like. A world supposing that choice can be limitless – because it's lost sight of the fact that the only limitless reality there is, isn't a thing to be owned, but a God to be praised and adored.

But consumerism is just a modern example of a problem that actually takes us back to the earliest centuries of Christianity. The writings of St Athanasius, for instance, address head-on a world-view where 'signs' are worshipped more than the God whose energising presence they 'signify'. And right there in the first years of the emerging Church, when Paul was preaching the Gospel in Lystra, people were getting this wrong: responding excitedly to the signs and miracles that happened whilst ignoring the continuing witness of God to his people to be found in the rhythm of the seasons and the fruits of creation.

Reading: Acts 14: 8-17

In Lystra there was a man sitting who could not use his feet and had never walked, for he had been crippled from birth. He listened to Paul as he was speaking. And Paul, looking at him intently and seeing that he had faith to be healed, said in a loud voice, 'Stand upright on your feet.' And the man sprang up and began to walk. When the crowds saw what Paul had done, they shouted in the Lyconian language, 'The gods have come down to us in human form!' Barnabas they called Zeus, and Paul they called Hermes, because he was the chief speaker. The priest of Zeus, whose temple was just outside the city, brought oxen and garlands to the gates; he and the crowds wanted to offer sacrifice. When the apostles Barnabas and Paul heard of it, they tore their clothes and rushed out into the crowd, shouting, 'Friends, why are you doing this? We are mortals just like you, and we bring you good news, that you should turn from these worthless things to the living God, who made the heaven and the earth and the sea and all that is in them. In past generations he allowed all the nations to follow their own ways; yet he has not left himself without a witness in doing good – giving you rains from heaven and fruitful seasons, and filling you with food and your hearts with joy.'

Rains from heaven and fruitful seasons. It doesn't sound much to be thankful for amidst the welter of choice Western consumerism has to offer. But try telling your average Ethiopian or Zimbabwean right now that these things aren't actually matters of life and death. Goodness, how we in the West need to readjust our priorities so that our Harvest praise of the earth's beauty, and the love of God in creation, over and around us, actually keys us into the divine dream of a world characterised not by greed but by sharing.

Choir: For the beauty of the earth, John Rutter

John Rutter's setting of Francis Pierpoint's hymn, For the beauty of the earth, takes us into our prayers.

We praise God for the beauty of the earth, the rhythm of the seasons and the cycle of renewal at the heart of all life.

As we give thanks for the richness of the resources we've been given to share, so we recognise the fragility of God's world: the damage done to the environment through human exploitation and the inequalities that result from human greed and wickedness.

We pray for communities affected by famine, natural disaster and conflict, where millions lack the basics of life. We pray especially for all reeling from the impact of the terrorist bombing in Islamabad, the injured and the bereaved. We remember the tens of thousands of children in China affected by tainted baby milk, the anxiety of parents and carers, and all who are seeking to limit this crisis.

As also we remember those in our own country affected by the credit crunch and rising prices, the turmoil in financial markets and the threat to jobs throughout our economy.

Give us wisdom as we chart a way forward. Recall us to your promise to provide for all our needs and invite us to seek only enough for each day, as we say the prayer your Son taught us: *Our Father ...*

As we join our prayers of thanksgiving and intercession to those of worshippers around the globe, so we sing of the Lord's goodness and bless his name.

Hymn: Sing of the Lord's goodness

As we sing of your goodness, Lord and Father of all wisdom, give us courage in our darkness, comfort in our sorrow, solace for the weary, and continue to bless and sustain us, this day and evermore. *Amen.*

19. To seek and to save: crippled

15 October 2008

Good morning.

Our theme this week on Daily Service is 'to seek and to save', and today we focus on a woman crippled by a psychological illness from the burden of which Jesus sets her free.

But let's be honest, such healing miracles are felt by many to be both perplexing and excluding, because in a world where there's so much sickness and suffering, why is it that some get better – some are healed – and not others, when what we all want and need is, as our first hymn puts it, cures for our ills, beauty for brokenness, hope for despair.

Hymn: Beauty for brokenness

God of the poor, friend of the weak, give us compassion, we pray: as you melt our cold hearts may the tears of healing grace that we shed bathe us in the ocean of your love. *Amen.*

Why her and not me? It's the child to parent, the child to teacher question that heralds the discussion of some supposed injustice in the playground or the home, or indeed the office. But it's also, if we're honest, the question that's never far from our own lips when we hear about someone else's good-fortune in contrast with our woes and worries, however slight in reality these may be. Of course, most of us are sophisticates when it comes to hiding this resentment, masking it with other seemingly more legitimate concerns. But eventually our burning resentment is unmasked, as it was when Jesus encountered a needy soul in the synagogue, and faced a backlash for helping her.

Reading: Luke 13: 10-17

Now Jesus was teaching in one of the synagogues on the Sabbath. And just then there appeared a woman with a spirit that had crippled her for eighteen years. She was bent over and was quite unable to stand up straight. When Jesus saw her, he called her over and said, 'Woman, you are set free from your ailment.' When he laid his hands on her, immediately she stood up straight and began praising God. But the leader of the synagogue, indignant because Jesus had cured on the Sabbath, kept saying to the crowd, 'There are six days on which work ought to be done; come on those days and be cured, and not on the Sabbath day.' But the Lord answered him and said, 'You hypocrites! Does not each of you on the Sabbath untie his ox or his donkey from the manger, and lead it away to give it water? And ought not this woman, a daughter of Abraham whom Satan bound for eighteen long years, be set free from this bondage on the Sabbath day?' When he said this, all his opponents were put to shame; and the entire crowd was rejoicing at all the wonderful things that he was doing.

If it hadn't been the wrong day of the week, it would have been something else that set the leader of the synagogue off. 'Why her and not me?' his heart was really crying out. But this masked itself as a leader's controlling, authoritarian tetchiness. Jesus, this Galilean upstart was on his territory, threatening the equilibrium and stability of synagogue life, flouting the rules – and, worst of all – doing good. I'm not going to stand for that he thought. Whatever next?

It's a depressing response of course but it's the sort of response that supposedly religious folk often make when the Spirit blows where she wills and produces effects not to be found in the religious leader's handbook!

But the resentful stuff – why's she been healed and not me? – which lurks just beneath the surface really isn't the place to start.

Some questions, as one of my theology professors used to remind me, are just stupid questions, simply the wrong ones to be asking.

Ask a different question, look sideways rather than straight on

– ask, for instance, what the metaphysical rather than the physical meaning to the story might be, or even its metaphorical meaning, and we realise that here is a narrative not so much about the crippling psychological imbalances of one woman, but about the crippling inadequacies of religious practitioners who can't recognise a good thing unless it happens to them.

But it's not just a story for religious folk of course. Look sideways at our society right now and we know that we are being made to realise the crippling inadequacy of market-driven capitalism, of a whole view and way of life founded on 'why her and not me' because it places my needs at its apex, at its centre, as goal and way.

How we need to respond to the heartfelt plea of our anthem, and come to God as we are, to be healed of all that cripples our lack of vision.

Choir: Just as I am, Bob Chilcott

Bob Chilcott's setting of Charlotte Eliot's hymn text, Just as I am, taking us into our prayers.

Just as we are, Lord, take us, break us and remake us in your image.

Give us the ability to see beyond the narrow confines of concern for self, family, party, church and nation.

Reform our selfishness, our concern to be measured by what we own rather than what we hold in common.

Transform our jealousy, our desire to denigrate others for their good-fortune, our self-indulgence about perceived slights and injustices.

Help us to look now on the poverty of vision that sets the acquisition of wealth as the measure of our humanity, when so many are materially and spiritually poor.

Use us to reach out to them and to all who live in places where the crippled, the conflict-ridden and the lost need your healing touch.

Guide us to re-establish the saving values of your kingdom as we say the words of the prayer your Son taught us: *Our Father ...*

As we seek to construct a vision of church, nation and world to transcend selfishness and bring healing for all, Come let us sing of a wonderful love, tender and true.

Hymn: Come let us sing

So may God's wonderful love, tender and true, abide in our hearts, lift us above envy, falsehood and pride, teach us to be humble and make us learners of the divine life, as God blesses us this day and evermore. *Amen.*

20. Tidings of comfort: a song of deliverance

10 December 2008

Good morning.

The Advent season is filled with tidings of comfort – our theme this week – which are hopefully also tidings of joy, challenge and inspiration. This morning Zechariah, a priest serving at the temple in Jerusalem, looks beyond the birth of his own son, John the Baptist, to the coming of another, who is the promised Saviour. And I guess that's always the challenge with prophetic tidings, to see within and beyond them the Christ whose glory is to fill the skies.

Hymn: Christ whose glory fills the skies

Fill me, radiancy divine, pierce the gloom of sin and grief, scatter the darkness of my unbelief and make me a channel for the bright beams of your love. *Amen.*

It's quite a transformation for Zechariah. He starts as a stuttering unbeliever who can't understand how his elderly wife Elizabeth could possibly have conceived a son. He's punished as a result and struck temporarily dumb. Until we reach the moment when his son is born, his speech returns, he names his child John, and instantly recognises that this boy isn't half so important as the one to whom he points.

One suspects that quite a lot of lived experience has got compressed here into a single story. But what a story of comfort and conversion it is: a story of Spirit-filled utterance transcending the past and bringing the longed-for future into the present.

Reading: Luke 1: 67-74

Then Zechariah was filled with the Holy Spirit and spoke this prophecy:

'Blessed be the Lord God of Israel, for he has looked favourably on his people and redeemed them.

He has raised up a mighty saviour for us in the house of his servant David, as he spoke through the mouth of his holy prophets from of old, that we would be saved from our enemies and from the hand of all who hate us.

Thus he has shown the mercy promised to our ancestors, and has remembered his holy covenant, the oath that he swore to our ancestor Abraham, to grant us that we, being rescued from the hands of our enemies, might serve him without fear.

We only hear a snatch there of the great song that pours forth from Zechariah's newly-opened mouth. The song known by its Latin name, Benedictus.

The first two chapters of Luke's Gospel, which tell the story of the births of John and Jesus, contain four songs of which Zechariah's is one. Mary sings when she meets Elizabeth, angels sing over Bethlehem, and Simeon sings in the temple when Jesus is presented to the religious authorities. And each song has an unmistakable note of joy.

But along with joy comes something a bit more demanding in each case. Yes, this Saviour will liberate us. Yes he will fulfil our story, realise the promises and hopes of our ancestors, but he will also deal with the root problem, with our enemies both within and without.

There's comfort here of course – as Bishop Sebastian Bakare from Harare in Zimbabwe reminded me during the recent Lambeth Conference.

This, he said, is the song we sing each morning in the Church's daily rhythm of prayer and praise, and with good reason, because we know God is with us and for us. He's our Father and comforter.

But, he continued, we also sing it because God's enemies hem us in on every side. And those enemies need converting to Christ.

That's an amazingly positive way of looking at the song as it resonates in such a difficult context: a statement to troubled people that speaks of comfort and challenge. And what results from its singing in trouble-filled Harare is exactly what the song suggested: a people serving God without fear, set free to proclaim God's message of peace even where terror reigns. Is our own Advent journey, I wonder, also leading us to be messengers of peace?

Choir: How beautiful upon the mountains, John Stainer

John Stainer's setting of Isaiah's vision of discipleship, How beautiful upon the mountains are the feet of him that bringeth good tidings, that publisheth peace. A vision which takes us into our prayers.

Choir chant: Wait for the Lord, Taizé

So we pray for courage to proclaim a message of peace amidst dark times, a message which calls for change of attitude, a conversion of the heart. A message which challenges our tendency to resort to conflict.

We pray particularly for all who seek to address issues of oppression, terrorism, and rule by mob violence, coercion or manipulation in our world, especially in Zimbabwe.

We pray for ourselves, that tidings of comfort will have a prophetic edge in our lives: when they see us comfort the afflicted as well as afflict the comfortable.

Choir chant: Wait for the Lord

We pray that together with brothers and sisters of faith and goodwill the world over we may realise that kingdom for the liberated for which Jesus taught us to pray, when we say: *Our Father ...*

So we pray that God will lead us all to find perfect freedom, unity, forgiveness and hope in Jesus Christ, as we sing the hymn, Praise to you, O Christ, our Saviour.

Hymn: Praise to you, O Christ

Bind us and unite us, Lord Jesus Christ; teach us and forgive us; bless us as instruments of your comfort, challenge and change, this day and evermore. *Amen.*

21. Christmas tidings – The Incarnation: the reflection of God's generosity – New Year's Eve

31 December 2008

Good morning.

To make an end is to make a beginning… the end is where we start from. Those teasing words from TS Eliot's Little Gidding seem good ones for the last day of 2008, the day that marks 'the turning of the year' as another poet Thomas Hardy describes it. Tomorrow we'll begin a new year with all its hopes and expectations. But for now we're drawing a line – at least metaphorically – and perhaps even trying to put a full stop. I don't know what the year's been like for you, but I guess it won't have been without its joys or sorrows.

Whatever our experience, however, the Christian faith teaches us that we must cultivate one response: thankfulness, not least for the amazing grace of the God who's led us through 2008 and always promises to lead us.

Hymn: Amazing grace

Lord of the years, we sing your praise for all that you have done to sustain us this past year. Thank you for the grace that's carried us through dangers, toils and snares, that's brought us thus far. Keep us in this grace as you lead us to our eternal home. *Amen.*

If you only say one prayer in your life make it 'thank you'. So said St Augustine – a man who knew a thing or two about life's ups and downs. A man who freely admits in his wonderful book, Confessions, that he'd frankly wasted quite a lot of his time either gratifying carnal desires or pursuing mistaken philosophies, until he sat in a garden, read St Paul, and was converted to Jesus. Would that it were that easy! Nonetheless, Confessions is an ideal book with which to see in the first few weeks of a new year.

But even though our minds have probably started turning to those somewhat dreaded New Year's resolutions, we're not of course there just yet. A good way to straddle this turning point however and to combine backward and forward looking glances is to take the advice of another of Africa's spiritual giants, Desmond Tutu. "When you sit at your desk in the morning … always work out who you should thank from the day before … and then send them a postcard." Having worked with the man they call the Arch, I'm lucky to have a stack of those postcards – all quite illegible of course since the Arch's handwriting is amongst the spindliest around! "But at least you knew I was probably saying something nice," he'd guffaw to his staff, when people complained they really couldn't read a word.

Whatever those postcards said, the message remains that characteristically biblical one: look back with thankfulness, see the hand of God.

Reading: Titus 3:3-7

For we ourselves were once foolish, disobedient, led astray, slaves to various passions and pleasures, passing our days in malice and envy, despicable, hating one another. But when the goodness and loving-kindness of God our Saviour appeared, he saved us, not because of any works of righteousness that we had done, but according to his mercy, through the water of rebirth and renewal by the Holy Spirit. This Spirit he poured out on us richly through Jesus Christ our Saviour, so that, having been justified by his grace, we might become heirs according to the hope of eternal life.

Mercy, grace, renewal … the Spirit's gifts poured out richly in our lives. If we were to write a postcard for each day in the year that's ending, could we find someone to thank for those gifts? Someone through whom God has spoken? For sure we'd trip over some days. As the Bible reminds us, the cross – sometimes a cross of our own making – is always there as a stumbling block to our smooth passage. But it doesn't stop our safe passage in an ultimate sense. Always, just round the corner there'll be some kind of resurrection, someone trying to bring us back to life again; that eternal life – 'aliveness' would be a better translation of the Greek – which St John's Gospel makes the mark of the Christian in this world, not simply the hope held out to us for the next, the world God so loved that he gave his only begotten Son, that whoso believeth in him should not perish but have everlasting life.

Choir: God so loved the world, John Stainer

John Stainer's setting of God so loved the World from his oratorio, Crucifixion, taking us into our prayers.

We pray with thankfulness for all that the last year has shown us of God's grace. We pray this especially if the year has been marked by grief or suffering, by pain or tribulation, by anxiety or heart-break. We pray it not because thankfulness is easy, but because we know your guiding hand, O Lord, bringing us safely thus far, bringing us alive again.

We pray with thankfulness for those issues which people have struggled to deal with in the field of international affairs: for the courage of political leaders in the face of the daunting challenges that have beset our financial markets or the fortitude of the oppressed in the face of tyranny in Zimbabwe.

We pray with thankfulness even when we recognise in our public or private lives failure to deal with complex situations: the rape of women in the war in the Democratic Republic of Congo or the lack of integrity in our own actions. We pray with thankfulness because we know that if we trust in your love, you will bring us to our senses, and bring us home.

So we accept the challenge of the words of Jesus as we say together: *Our Father …*

We acknowledge the reign of the one to whom all thanks is owed, and whose generosity transforms our lives: Hail to the Lord's Anointed! Great David's greater Son.

Hymn: Hail to the Lord's anointed

From age to age, from year to year, from day to day we pray that the tide of time will never remove your covenant, O God, as you bless us with your Love. *Amen.*

22. Reconcile your people: faith and hope founded on God

21 January 2009

Good morning from Washington DC, where it's 4.45 am and the last revellers from the many Inaugural Balls and parties here are heading to bed as early-bird staff members in President Barack Obama's team wake to the work of a new US administration.

There probably won't be much time for the President to reflect on the iconic significance of his inauguration. But for those of us who were present – or who clustered around televisions, laptops or radios to watch and listen to yesterday's swearing-in and inaugural address – there's just so much on which to ponder. So much that, as the new President has often acknowledged, the only place to start is with those four words that end the oath of office: 'so help me God'. For whatever we face each day it's in God's strength that we must trust, on him that all our hopes are founded.

Hymn: All my hope on God is founded, sung by the Cambridge Singers.

Lord Jesus Christ, you call us to follow you and unite us in one community and fellowship so that we may not fall. Protect those chosen as our leaders, that strengthened by our service and sacrifice their gifts may enrich and extend the reach of your eternal kingdom. Amen.

As President Obama took his hand off the Bible that Abraham Lincoln had used in his inaugural in 1861, he began to address as expectant a world as any American president has perhaps ever addressed. With his own country and indeed countries everywhere, experiencing what the President referred to as a widely-acknowledged financial crisis, to say nothing of other conflicts and challenges, I cannot imagine what it must feel like to bear that weight of responsibility. But as he turned to face towards the Washington Monument, the millions lining the National Mall, and the billions beyond them listening in every corner of the globe, I couldn't help being struck by the vulnerability of what had happened moments before, when a clearly overawed Chief Justice changed the word order of the oath, no doubt causing the new President a degree of discomfort. But as his own words soared towards those of us who had braved the bitter chill of a winter's morning to force the spring, by huddling together in such numbers, his reassuring smile to the Chief Justice made one of his central points: the need for mutual support.

The atmosphere amongst the almost two million people present in Washington's National Mall was electric. But what made President Obama's inauguration particularly moving was the unity of spirit that saw everyone believing that they could be the change they wanted. It was as if the renewal that he was encouraging in American society – an embracing extension of the American dream – was somehow reaching out to the whole world, not arrogantly to seek dominance but with genuine humility to seek partnership that can become friendship.

And it's that deep desire for reconciliation that of course lies at the heart of the Global Week of Prayer that Christians are keeping right now, as we seek that unity which is God's will for the whole of creation, a unity which President Obama so frequently emphasises in a three-word affirmation: we are one.

Jonathan Reiber, a young American who's been a foreign and defence policy aid to the Obama Campaign, reminds us now that this reality expresses itself in the oneness of community we name as God – whose truth calls forth mutual love to sow imperishable, eternal seeds of goodness.

Reading: 1 Peter 1: 19-25

Jesus was destined before the foundation of the world, but was revealed at the end of the ages for your sake. Through him you have come to trust in God, who raised him from the dead and gave him glory, so that your faith and hope are set on God. Now that you have purified your souls by your obedience to the truth so that you have genuine mutual love, love one another deeply from the heart. You have been born anew, not of perishable but of imperishable seed, through the living and enduring word of God. For 'All flesh is like grass and all its glory like the flower of grass. The grass withers, and the flower falls, but the word of the Lord endures for ever.' That word is the good news that was announced to you.

The good news in President Obama's words was a universal invitation to inhabit a story that's captivated people everywhere for thousands of years. This is the eternal narrative of liberation that sees Moses lead God's people to the edge of the promised land, but that now requires us to go with Joshua and to cross the Jordan towards the fulfilment of our calling – the spirit of unity and hope moving in our hearts, urging us on, and helping us to conquer all our fears.

African-American Spiritual: Ev'ry time I feel the Spirit, sung by The Florida Agricultural & Mechanical University Concert Choir.

The only thing we have to fear is fear itself. So said Franklin Roosevelt, one of President Obama's heroes, in his inaugural address in 1933, when the world faced a financial crisis similar to now. To which our response, as the President put it yesterday, echoing another of his heroes, Abraham Lincoln, needs to be, "Let it be told in the future, that in the depth of winter, the city and country alarmed at one common danger came forth to meet it," an invitation which takes us into our prayers.

We pray amidst our financial crisis for the ability to re-imagine structures so that they may serve the common good.

We pray in the light of so much mistrust of peoples and institutions that we may extend hands of friendship to unclench fists of fear, and may have the grace to recognise when our hands must first be unclenched.

We pray amidst the severe conflicts of our time, not least between Israeli and Palestinian, for the courage to define ourselves by what we build and not by what we destroy.

So in the midst of winter we face common dangers and opportunities as we embrace the reality of God's kingdom, saying: *Our Father ...*

We have a long way to walk to realise the dream of that kingdom but we can do it by making the spirit of an old American hymn our own: I once was lost, but now am found, was blind, but through God's grace can now I see.

Hymn: Amazing Grace, sung by Jessye Norman.

So we give thanks for the amazing grace that has brought us thus far in our journey, as we pray that God will always bless us with this grace, and bring us home. Amen.

23. Sight can enhance our spiritual journeys: Zacchaeus sees Jesus

3 March 2009

Choir: The eyes of all, Ian Tracey

Good morning.

Following the words of the opening music, our theme this first week of Lent considers how sight can enhance our spiritual journeying and particularly how we see with the eye of the heart. Why? Because this kind of seeing is transforming: it's good news, something to shout about from the mountain tops.

Hymn: Go tell it on the mountain, arranged John Rutter

As God uses us to speak for him and to touch the lives of people near and far, so may he school us to see with his divine eyes of compassion and love. *Amen.*

When I was living and working in central London, I often used to take one of our sons to the latest exhibition at the National Gallery. One afternoon, it was the turn of our then three-year-old Gregory. And the exhibition in question consisted in works all by Raphael.

I'll always remember descending the steps to the basement of the National Gallery, not only for the long queue but for the looks of horror on the faces of those around us. All of them no doubt thinking why on earth has this mad priest brought a talkative and excitable three-year-old to see works by Raphael?

Indeed, the looks hardened as we reached the gallery.

Greg was still chattering away but then as he confronted the first painting talk gave way to total silence.

And the looks also began to change as people saw a little figure move slowly from painting to painting, pausing to drink in light and shade, colours and figures and backgrounds.

I wasn't myself paying much attention to the paintings. I was simply watching Greg and the reactions of other people as he would tug at my arm and whisper some observation or other.

Eventually we came to the most crowded bit of the exhibition which contained the smallest – and perhaps most famous of the works there – The Madonna of the Pinks.

Craning to see it, the index finger of Greg's left hand was soon pointing to something he'd noticed.

"Look, Daddy," he said. "See that window. See the chink in the wood."

An art connoisseur nearby gasped audibly and walked straight over to the two of us.

"That's remarkable, he's spotted the one thing most people miss, the thing that creates the painting's perspective and drama … the detail that intentionally lacks perfection which is that chink in the window sill."

"How amazing to be taught that by a child," he added. But it's not actually that amazing. All of us possess the ability to see the deepest truths, the person who lights up a room or a roadside, the little man up a tree who really needs an encouraging word and the healing hand of transformation. It's just most of the time we're too blinded, in words of the poet Tagore, by 'delusion and dust', to notice the most obvious and the most telling details.

Reading: Luke 19: 1-9

Jesus entered Jericho and was passing through it. A man was there named Zacchaeus; he was a chief tax-collector and was rich. He was trying to see who Jesus was, but on account of the crowd he could not, because he was short in stature. So he ran ahead and climbed a syca-more tree to see him, because he was going to pass that way. When Jesus came to the place, he looked up and said to him, 'Zacchaeus,

hurry and come down; for I must stay at your house today.' So he
hurried down and was happy to welcome him. All who saw it began to
grumble and said, 'He has gone to be the guest of one who is a sinner.'
Zacchaeus stood there and said to the Lord, 'Look, half of my posses-
sions, Lord, I will give to the poor; and if I have defrauded anyone of
anything, I will pay back four times as much.' Then Jesus said to him,
'Today salvation has come to this house, because he too is a son of
Abraham. For the Son of Man came to seek out and to save the lost.'

Something about Jesus instinctively captivated Zacchaeus,
enough to persuade him to shin up a tree in the hope of catching
the Master's attention. This special something was met and
matched by a God whose seeing went straight to the heart of a
man who needed not just to be helped down from a tree but out of
the hole he'd dug for himself. One kind of seeing led to another
and salvation dawned. But it all stemmed from a gift of sight
which is really a gift of insight, a gift that's ours for the taking, if
we train ourselves to be attentive to the smallest details about our
contexts and our neighbours.

Choir: See what love, Felix Mendelssohn-Bartholdy

See what love the Father hath bestowed on us. Setting words
from the First Epistle of John in Mendelssohn's oratorio, St Paul,
words which take us into our prayers.

We bless you Lord for the love that you bestow upon us, helping us to know that you are present in the world.

We pray for grace to discern this presence more deeply: to see
the neediness in the eyes that meet us on the street corners of our
cities or to sense the hopelessness in hands outstretched for a crust
of bread.

We express sorrow for those ways in which our moral blindness blights the lives of others: for our double-standards, the
oppression that we ignore in one place whilst we criticise it in

another and for the delusion and dust with which we so often fill our lives.

Help us, like Zacchaeus, to make reparations for our shortcomings, and to see with the eye of the heart as we embrace the truth of St Teresa of Avila's prayer:

Christ has no body on earth but ours, no hands but ours, no feet but ours. Ours are the eyes through which he is to look with compassion on the world. Ours are the feet with which he is to go about doing good, and ours are the hands with which he is to bless us now. *Amen.*

So let us pray that we will see and embrace the fullness of the promised kingdom as we say together: *Our Father ...*

Knowing the journey we must walk to have sight turned to insight, we acknowledge the one who alone can lead us: God is love, let heaven adore him, God is love, let earth rejoice!

Hymn: God is love

May the spiritual blindness that afflicts us and the sin that weighs us down be transformed by God's all-seeing and all-loving presence, this day and evermore. *Amen.*

24. Holy Week: hearing the cry of betrayal

7 April 2009

Choir: Stay with me, Jacques Berthier

Good morning.

Watch and pray. Those three simple words sung to a chant from the Taizé community in France introduce the narrative context for today's Holy Week theme: hearing the cry of betrayal. Because they take us to the Garden of Gethsemane, and to the lone figure of a man desperate for support as he faces betrayal, suffering and death in order to be servant king of all.

Hymn: From heaven you came, helpless babe

Teach us, good Lord, to serve you as you deserve: to give and not to count the cost, to fight and not to heed the wounds, to toil and not to seek for rest, to labour and not to ask for any reward, save the joy of knowing that we do your will. Amen.

St Ignatius Loyola

Words don't always enable us to get to the heart of things. And though – in a minute – we shall hear some words from Matthew's Gospel which describe both the loneliness of the Christ who looks for support and finds none, and the treachery of the moment when he's betrayed with a kiss from Judas Iscariot, we can best approach these twin stories from a painting that holds them together. It's a famous depiction of the Agony in the Garden, as it's called, which hangs in the National Gallery in London, and it's by the fifteenth century Italian artist, Giovanni Bellini. At its heart, facing heavenwards and kneeling behind a rock is the praying Christ, hands clasped deliberately yet gently together in prayer. Beyond him to

the right the viewer sees a winding road towards the city of Jerusalem – a road along which a crucifixion happens 'outside the city
wall' as the old hymn says, but one that's also the road to glory: to
the heavenly city where all shall be well. To the left and in the distance soldiers come, led by Judas. A motley band, they hurry
along and are about to cross a narrow bridge as if they're walking
a tight rope. Perhaps we hope that they'll fall off and won't fulfil
their awful intention to betray the one who prays serenely at the
heart of the picture. But we know in reality that this serenity is
going to be shattered. It's already been shattered by the three disciples in the foreground just behind Jesus, whose contorted bodies
sleep at odd angles to him, to emphasise their betrayal. Their Lord
and Master's in fact the only true vertical in the scene, save for the
angel top right who offers him the cup of suffering – a chalice of
wine – which he must accept.

It's a haunting dramatisation of the scene we hear now from
Matthew's Gospel, and which invites us to ponder those times
when we've betrayed God's will by going it alone, or our neighbours by refusing to accept their neediness even to empathise with
their thoughts and feelings.

Reading: Matthew 26: 40-50

*Then Jesus came to the disciples and found them sleeping; and he said
to Peter, 'So, could you not stay awake with me one hour? Stay awake
and pray that you may not come into the time of trial the spirit indeed
is willing, but the flesh is weak.' Again he went away for the second
time and prayed, 'My Father, if this cannot pass unless I drink it,
your will be done.' Again he came and found them sleeping, for their
eyes were heavy. So leaving them again, he went away and prayed for
the third time, saying the same words. Then he came to the disciples
and said to them, 'Are you still sleeping and taking your rest? See, the
hour is at hand, and the Son of Man is betrayed into the hands of sinners. Get up, let us be going. See, my betrayer is at hand.'
While he was still speaking, Judas, one of the twelve, arrived; with
him was a large crowd with swords and clubs, from the chief priests*

and the elders of the people. Now the betrayer had given them a sign, saying, 'The one I will kiss is the man; arrest him.' At once he came up to Jesus and said, 'Greetings, Rabbi!' and kissed him. Jesus said to him, 'Friend, do what you are here to do.' Then they came and laid hands on Jesus and arrested him.

Of course the tension in the scene is always going to resolve itself on the side of the angels. But this isn't some cost-free, happy ending. This resolution of the very sin first committed in a garden, and now corrected through the agony of a garden prayer, takes us back along Bellini's winding road to another place of desolation: a cross.

Choir: In a garden, man became heir, Johann Sebastian Bach (edited Ian Tracey)

That chorale by Johann Sebastian Bach, one of the composers – in his Passion music – to have penetrated most deeply the meaning of betrayal, and cross, and the hope they win for us, leads us into our prayers.

We pray for all who feel betrayed by the inequalities of our world: the richness enjoyed by so many at the expense of the poverty of millions; the peace and security enjoyed by the privileged behind walls which exclude and marginalise.

Choir chant: Stay with me ...

We pray for all who betray their loved ones by cheating on them, undermining them, slighting or abusing them. May each perpetrator and victim know the transforming power of Christ's cross.

Choir chant: Stay with me ...

We pray for all at this time who face a difficult road of acceptance. Acceptance of who they are, or of the disease with which they must live, or the suffering that they must endure, especially those caught up in the Italian earthquake. Send them an angel to bring them your comfort and healing in body, mind or spirit.

Choir chant: Stay with me ...

We seek grace to accept God's will in our lives, however challenging this may be, as we say the prayer our Saviour taught us: Our Father ...

So we pray for renewed strength whatever we face on our journey as we turn to Christ, our sure comfort in trouble and distress.

Hymn: All ye who seek a comfort sure

Wash my wounds in your blood, O Lord: bless and inspire me with new grace and hope: a heart to do your will, this day and evermore. Amen.

25. Eternal life

27 May 2009

Good morning.

This week our theme's 'eternal life'. But immediately we say those two words in English we bang our heads up against a real problem of translation. For the Greek which actually gets translated as eternal life, might more literally be rendered as 'endlessly lively.'

I guess that's the sort of phrase we'd come out with when we'd been looking after a friend's exhausting toddler – or even one of our own for that matter! For whilst eternal life conjures up rather passive images of a distant heaven, 'endlessly lively' suggests something much more dynamic, perhaps even rather too hot to handle! This is where our first hymn, Amazing grace, comes into its own because it speaks of a quality of living – the eternal pulse of God's grace within us now – propelling us towards our eternal home.

Hymn: Amazing grace

Living Lord, as you draw us to the life of endless perfection which is the fullness of your eternal kingdom, make us 'endlessly lively' in singing your praises each and every day. Amen.

I'll always remember the first time I learnt what those two words 'eternal life' really mean. I was in the Sheldonian Theatre in Oxford as a second year undergraduate, one of about a thousand sitting spell-bound as a man, small in stature but a giant in wisdom, gave just about as virtuosic an exposition of the Christian faith as you'd ever hear. Recently retired as bishop of Winchester, John V Taylor, one of the great Anglican theologians of the twentieth century, was giving a mission to Oxford University that was unforgettable to the students there of my generation. The

Sheldonian was in fact packed to the rafters for five nights as he addressed his theme: a matter of life and death. And what was most compelling was the sense in which the medium was the message, his own endlessly alert and lively presentation being absolutely infectious. Many of us literally caught the spirit of what he said and the Spirit of God behind it, calling each of us to discern how God was working his purpose out in our own lives. I remember he included the words we're about to hear from John chapter 3, and as he did so he emphasised the choice they invited us to make between life and death, the deadliness of routine religion or the liveliness of life in the Spirit.

Reading: John 3: 11-17

'Very truly, I tell you, we speak of what we know and testify to what we have seen; yet you do not receive our testimony. If I have told you about earthly things and you do not believe, how can you believe if I tell you about heavenly things? No one has ascended into heaven except the one who descended from heaven, the Son of Man. And just as Moses lifted up the serpent in the wilderness, so must the Son of Man be lifted up, that whoever believes in him may have eternal life. 'For God so loved the world that he gave his only Son, so that everyone who believes in him may not perish but may have eternal life. 'Indeed, God did not send the Son into the world to condemn the world, but in order that the world might be saved through him.

Familiarity is said to breed contempt, but I think in the religious realm it tends to breed indifference. We just don't hear the dynamism of the words – and, more importantly, feel the electricity of the experience that's on offer through them because – well – we've heard it all before. And in the passage we've just heard it all hinges again on how we translate the original Greek. For when John says that God gave his Son, he uses the verb didowmi – which means to give in a completely unforced, self-emptying way. Later in the Gospel it becomes paradidowmi – when Jesus hands over his life in love for the world. And that's what each of us is to discover about God's purpose for our lives, that as God brings us to life so he wants us to hand ourselves over to that stream of love which brings the whole cosmos to life.

Choir: God so loved the world, John Stainer

John Stainer's setting from his oratorio, Crucifixion, of those words from John's Gospel, which take us into our prayers.

We pray for those places in the world which most need the liveliness of the Spirit to heal, to restore and to renew. We pray especially at this time for the peoples of North and South Korea.

We pray that all who serve in public life may be alive to the way in which God is working his purpose through them.

We pray for all who have become immune to the reality of God's kingdom here on earth as in heaven.

Using the words that Jesus taught us, we pray that the gift of this life may dawn for each of us, as we say: Our Father …

So as we look to the triumph of God's grace in our lives we join with thousands of tongues to sing our great Redeemer's praise.

Hymn: O for a thousand tongues

As the dead in body, mind or spirit receive new life from your hands, O Lord, may each of us be blessed in seeking to spread the good news of eternal life, in furthering your healing work, and in spreading the honour of your name, this day and evermore. Amen.

26. Healing: through our relationship with God

22 October 2009

Good Morning.

Last week I was in Bosnia-Herzegovina, as one of a dozen Christians and Muslims pondering different aspects of the theme which we're exploring in this week's daily services: healing. Today we reflect on what may be learnt about healing through our relationship with God.

Sometimes Christians are accused of being just a bit too 'pie in the sky when you die' in their thinking. Putting up with suffering and evil – not doing much to stand up to them – because, well, there's always the fairy land prize of heaven: the place where all the miseries of this world are ultimately reconciled. But our first hymn counters such woolly thinking very boldly. We love God not because we hope to escape hell and head for heaven. We love God because his very being and nature is reconciling love.

Hymn: My God, I love thee

Teach us, O Lord, to persevere with patience in our efforts to make peace so that, embracing the cost of your self-emptying love, the whole world may be healed. *Amen.*

It's all very well to assert the Christian message that God is self-emptying, reconciling love. But what does this sloganised truth look like on the ground, and in a place where the conflict's been so deep and desperate that the lie of the slogan can never last for long.

Bosnia-Herzegovina, on the frontier between Eastern and Western Europe, Eastern and Western Christianity, the place that has known the Austro-Hungarian and the Ottoman Empires, a region where Serbs, Croats and Bosniaks, Orthodox, Catholics and Muslims have lived for centuries – and sometimes fought each other: where better to test any pious talk about healing than this place?

Where indeed, when you arrive at Sarajevo airport and the first thing to greet you, beyond the fencing, are the holes in the walls of concrete flats caused by shelling during the terrible civil war of the 1990s.

It was a tough start, and the week was tough, as I encountered hurts and prejudices entrenched down the centuries. But meeting Bosnians of every ethnic and religious background, I nonetheless couldn't help hearing echoes – however faint – of the words we listen to now from St Paul's Epistle to the Romans.

Reading: Romans 5: 1-10

Therefore, since we are justified by faith, we have peace with God through our Lord Jesus Christ, through whom we have obtained access to this grace in which we stand; and we boast in our hope of sharing the glory of God. And not only that, but we also boast in our sufferings, knowing that suffering produces endurance, and endurance produces character, and character produces hope, and hope does not disappoint us, because God's love has been poured into our hearts through the Holy Spirit that has been given to us. For while we were still weak, at the right time Christ died for the ungodly. Indeed, rarely will anyone die for a righteous person – though perhaps for a good person someone might actually dare to die. But God proves his love for us in that while we still were sinners Christ died for us. Much more surely then, now that we have been justified by his blood, will we be saved through him from the wrath of God. For if while we were enemies, we were reconciled to God through the death of his Son, much more surely, having been reconciled, will we be saved by his life.

There's nothing cheap about the grace Paul advocates, and nothing pious either. For him, the hard slog of the cross – the reconciling activity of God lived out in our own lives – consists in suffering endured, character built, hope snatched from the debris of conflict, a hope that does not disappoint us, because it pours God's love into our hearts through the Holy Spirit.

And when I sat in a school in Tuzla, talking with a seventeen-year-old Muslim, Amer, I saw the fruits of this hard-won grace in a way I've rarely seen them before.

We chatted for quite a while and then I asked Amer what he thought was the most important lesson he'd learnt in his life.

He looked me straight in the eye and replied: "That the greatest power in the world is the strength of forgiveness."

"Where did that come from?" I asked, blown away by what he was saying. "From deep within me," he gently asserted.

I discovered later from one of his teachers that his family had been deeply scarred by the war of the 1990s so Amer's journey to healing and forgiveness must have been a very long one indeed.

Which was how, in the faith of a young Muslim, God showed me again one of the central truths that Christians proclaim: which is that we can't be healed through the force of our own character; only if we truly depend on God, love him with our whole heart – discover him, like Amer, in the depths of our being – may we experience the reconciling, transforming grace that changes everything.

Choir: If ye love me, Thomas Tallis

If ye love me, the music by Thomas Tallis, setting words from John chapter 14, words which take us into our prayers.

Let us pray that our love of God, however weak, will lead us to know the spirit of truth and peace in our lives.

Let us pray for this spirit especially in places like Bosnia--Herzegovina where people in all communities carry memories which are so hard to bear.

Let us give thanks for those whose peace-making and reconciling skills bring hope amidst sorrow and despair, especially those who combat the scourge of racism in our society.

And let us recall all for whom healing and reconciliation seem distant possibilities at this time.

Choir chant: My peace I leave you, Taizé

Let us pray a special blessing on all situations of conflict as we say the prayer that proclaims the reconciliation of earth and heaven in the words that Jesus taught us: *Our Father ...*

So we turn in faith and trust to God the source of all reconciliation, as we sing the ancient psalm, The Lord's my shepherd, to music by Stuart Townend.

Hymn: The Lord's my shepherd

As your endless mercy leads us, Lord, to feast where all are one in your love, so we pray that your blessing may be with us this day and evermore. *Amen.*

27. People on the edge of the action (Lent): Mary

16 March 2010

Good morning.

Being on the edge of the action – our theme today – offers a vantage point like no other. Zacchaeus up a tree, a blind man on a road, a centurion at the foot of a cross. All are in one sense peripheral to the central action. Yet it's invariably these people in the Gospel who are the first to understand the message, indeed pretty much the only ones to get it.

That says interesting things about the relationship of outside and inside. And the person we're thinking about this week – Jesus's mother Mary – is pivotal in this regard. Let's picture her now as we sing our Gathering song: Here in this place.

Song: Here in this place

As Gospel light once shone through a woman, marginal to the centres of power and influence, so we pray, Lord, that it may shine in us as you gather us in and make us your own. *Amen.*

I returned a few weeks ago from three months, lecturing and writing on sabbatical in Cape Town, so I think I know fairly immediately what being on the edge feels like.

You resist the temptation to read all the emails and follow the narrative of your day job too closely – so you're out of the loop – which in many ways is wonderfully liberating. But as you return you realise that it means you're a bit out of touch with where everyone is. You can easily feel and react defensively because life carries on and you haven't been part of it. In a way you've become an outsider. But you also see things perhaps with a sharpness insiders can rarely achieve which is equally liberating and defensive-making too.

It's complex, and as you get sucked back into the email and meetings vortex which is life in the contemporary church, the conflicting emotions and reactions jostle pretty uneasily.

That's actually what life was like for Mary. She'd brought the boy up, set him on his path, seen him shine in the local synagogue, and then she'd begun to become more of an outsider – as all mothers do, when their children grow up.

She'd heard about his itinerant life-style. Some said he was doing odd things, even that he was out of his mind. She was worried. From her perspective it looked like he'd lost the plot. She could no longer bear to be on the edge of his life. For her peace of mind she needed to be back at the centre.

So she turned up out of the blue as our reading from Mark chapter 3 informs us.

Reading: Mark 3: 31-35

Then his mother and his brothers came; and standing outside, they sent to him and called him. A crowd was sitting around him; and they said to him, 'Your mother and your brothers and sisters are outside, asking for you.' And he replied, 'Who are my mother and my brothers?' And looking at those who sat around him, he said, 'Here are my mother and my brothers! Whoever does the will of God is my brother and sister and mother.'

Ouch. That wasn't the reaction Mary wanted. It must have hurt like hell to be put in her place so harshly. But what sounds at first like rejection isn't meant to be, in the evangelist Mark's brusque style.

Jesus knows that he's been causing trouble. He knows this must have worried his mother. But he's saying that only when you're fully on the inside of discipleship will any of this trouble make sense and be seen for what it really is: a sign of God's dawning kingdom.

Since in the words of the traditional American song we hear now, nobody knows the trouble that Mary sees except the Son who started it, and who alone understands and transforms it.

Choir: Nobody knows the trouble I've seen Lord

Bob Chilcott's arrangement of Nobody knows the trouble I've seen Lord, taking us into our prayers.

We pray for all mothers who feel marginal in the lives of their children. For all who sense that they have lost their loved ones to addiction or dependency, to violence or criminality.

We pray for all who feel rejected by those close to them and who cannot get beyond the pain of the words spoken to understand the real needs being expressed.

We give thanks for the many agencies and individuals who seek to support people in such circumstances.

We rejoice today at the news from Pakistan that Sahil Saheed has been found and will soon be returned to his family in Oldham.

We pray that we may have the courage to be drawn deeper inside the mystery of God's grace as we say the prayer that he taught us: *Our Father …*

So we celebrate the way in which for Christ there can be no outsiders since in him there is no east or west.

Hymn: In Christ there is no east or west

Make us one, Lord, in your fellowship of love. Unite us throughout the whole wide earth and bless us with your grace, now and always. *Amen.*

28. Love one another (Maundy Thursday)

1 April 2010

Good morning.

In the Church's keeping of Holy Week we've reached the day of Jesus's last meal with his disciples, the meal in which he gives them a new commandment – "mandatum novum", as the Latin runs – that they love one another as he has loved them, a commandment he turns into a parable by washing his friends' feet.

'Mandatum novum' of course gives us the name of the day, Mandatum, Maundy Thursday. It's the day when Her Majesty The Queen gives Maundy money to people who've shown Christ-like service to the community – this year she distributes the money in Derby Cathedral.

And it's the day when Christians worldwide acknowledge Christ's love, 'vast as the ocean' filling their lives with grace.

Hymn: Here is love

Lord Jesus, as you washed the feet of your disciples, teaching them a new commandment and sealing this with a kiss: pour your love into our hearts, that our lives may become channels of your loving service, and fountains of transforming grace. *Amen.*

"I see you're the BBC's April fool, this year" a priest colleague of mine wryly observed as he scanned the list of Daily Service presenters for this week. Until he'd pointed out that I was presenting today on April 1st I hadn't made the connection. But – beyond my friend's black humour – the coincidence of April Fools Day and Maundy Thursday is actually a brilliant one. For from Paul's epistles – the earliest Christian writings – disciples, one and all, were encouraged to see themselves as 'fools for Christ'.

So what does this mean?

Is it the case that we must ape the caricature BBC vicar of the Derek Nimmo variety or follow Dot Cotton's somewhat over-literalist brand of Christianity and 'make fools of ourselves'?

Must Christians be buffoons because of the holy word-games too often played, the 'rarified' language we too often speak? – which may make sense on the inside of faith but which so many laugh at not out of disdain but because they're nervous: they simply don't understand what we're saying most of the time.

Or must we be 'fools for Christ' in a rather more profound way? And if so, how do we discover what it takes?

An answer seems to form on this Maundy Thursday with a young rabbi prepared to forsake the status of his office and wash feet.

This appears foolish to a world obsessed with status and position: a world that judges people by what they wear and own and drive.

It develops on a Friday with a man prepared to sacrifice everything for his beliefs – to be as recklessly foolish for the sake of truth as it's possible to be. A man prepared to look a fool and a failure for the sake of good.

It plays itself out further on a Saturday when there's nothing more to be said and believers look foolish because they've run out of answers and must simply wait and hope.

Just as it's crystallised on a Sunday when what seems at first a foolish tall story whispered around an empty tomb suddenly proves itself to be the narrative for which the whole world's been waiting.

How the foolishness of the cross becomes the wisdom of God: that's the movement on which the whole of Holy Week hinges. And it's a movement that can only be made by those who know what true love is.

Reading: John 13: 31b-35

Jesus said, 'Now the Son of Man has been glorified, and God has been glorified in him. If God has been glorified in him, God will also glorify him in himself and will glorify him at once. Little children, I am with you only a little longer. You will look for me; and as I said to the Jews so now I say to you, "Where I am going, you cannot come." I give you a new commandment, that you love one another. Just as I have loved you, you also should love one another. By this everyone will know that you are my disciples, if you have love for one another.'

Choir: A new commandment I give unto you

Let us pray.

As we recall the brokenness of our world, the places where violence and conflict reign, the arguments that rage between nations and cultures, the misunderstandings between faiths and world views, so we pray for the gift of love.

For that perfect love which casts out fear and which enables communities to grow in peace as they foster mutual respect and understanding.

For that self-giving love which creates real space for listening and dialogue.

For that generous love which seeks not its own satisfaction but the common good.

As we pray that our own attempts to love may be made with integrity and humility, so we express our sorrow for our failures to love and to serve.

O God of love, we ask you to give us love; love in our thinking, love in our speaking, love in our doing, and love in the hidden places of our souls; love of those who find it hard to bear with us;

love of those with whom we work, and love of those with whom we take our ease; that so at length we may be worthy to dwell with you, who are eternal love. *Amen.*

William Temple

Looking to the fullness of the kingdom of love Jesus promises all who follow him we say the words that he taught us:
Our Father ...

So we marvel at the love which transforms us and makes us whole: What kind of love is this that gave itself for me?

Song: What kind of love is this?

May the love of the Lord Jesus draw us to himself; may the power of the Lord Jesus strengthen us in his service; may the joy of the Lord Jesus fill our souls. May God almighty, the Father, the Son, and the Holy Spirit, bless us, and remain with us always. *Amen.*

29. The Holy Spirit: inspiring the Church

26 May 2010

Good morning.

This week, following the feast of Pentecost – Whitsunday as it's also called – we're reflecting on the being and nature of the Holy Spirit. And today we're thinking about how the Spirit inspires and energises. But to be inspired or energised of course we have to have an image of the Holy Spirit. Our first song hints at some familiar territory in this regard. Let's allow its words and music to get us thinking what our images of the Spirit might be: Holy Spirit, Lord of light!

Hymn: Holy Spirit, Lord of light

Descend, O Holy Spirit, with your seven-fold gifts of grace. Comfort and disturb us through the power of your presence. *Amen.*

At Blackburn Cathedral, where I work, we celebrated Pentecost with a festival of preaching which also marked the fiftieth anniversary of the College of Preachers. It seemed an appropriate thing to do since the very first sermon in the life of the Christian Church was preached at Pentecost by Peter. But Peter's words were uttered in response to a remarkable occurrence which is often glossed over in the ancient language of the sort of song we sang a few moments ago. Western Christianity tends to fear the Spirit's liberating and unsettling power. We Western Christians seem to wish for a rather more planned and strategic intervention of grace, the kind that a gentle dove might bring in its beak, on a scroll perhaps on which would be printed a well-crafted mission statement with outputs, outcomes and even an accompanying business plan.

But the first Pentecost was a little more chaotic than that. And as I stood in the transept of the cathedral before the service on Sunday one of my colleagues said rather excitedly to me: next year we're going to have twelve people speaking in different languages to start this service off – in our congregation we have people who speak roughly thirty different languages. Much more like the first Pentecost, as we'll hear now.

Reading: Acts 2: 1-13

When the day of Pentecost had come, they were all together in one place. And suddenly from heaven there came a sound like the rush of a violent wind, and it filled the entire house where they were sitting. Divided tongues, as of fire, appeared among them, and a tongue rested on each of them. All of them were filled with the Holy Spirit and began to speak in other languages, as the Spirit gave them ability.

Now there were devout Jews from every nation under heaven living in Jerusalem. And at this sound the crowd gathered and was bewildered, because each one heard them speaking in the native language of each. Amazed and astonished, they asked, 'Are not all these who are speaking Galileans? And how is it that we hear, each of us, in our own native language? Parthians, Medes, Elamites, and residents of Mesopotamia, Judea and Cappadocia, Pontus and Asia, Phrygia and Pamphylia, Egypt and the parts of Libya belonging to Cyrene, and visitors from Rome, both Jews and proselytes, Cretans and Arabs—in our own languages we hear them speaking about God's deeds of power.' All were amazed and perplexed, saying to one another, 'What does this mean?' But others sneered and said, 'They are filled with new wine.'

Violent wind and fire, amazement, astonishment and seeming drunkenness. It doesn't much sound like Sunday morning in any church that I know. But it's that kind of upheaval that the spirit induces. "Forget doves," said our preacher at Blackburn – who'd come all the way from Bury St Edmunds for the preaching festival. "At the centre of our cathedral we have a wolf..." Most cathedrals and churches have one of those I thought to myself, prowling about seeking whom to devour – but I resisted the temptation to shout that out, as Canon Vernon went on to tell us how in the legend of St Edmund a wolf had protected his decapitated head, and how a wolf seeking after its prey is in fact a much more appropriate image of a God who desires us to submit to his will for our lives, his will for the whole of creation, than the innocuous cooing of a dove. It was arresting stuff that made me think how much I prefer to domesticate God in the controlled flutterings of a bird rather than confront a God who could – if we call on him – quench the barrenness of both the physical and spiritual landscapes of our world.

Song: Send us the rain, Lord

Send us the rain, Lord, taking us into our prayers.

Let us pray that the arresting grace of God may transform those places of darkness and division in our world.

And that the energising presence of the Spirit may expose sin and evil as it sets the suffering and the oppressed free.

Let us pray that the enlightening truth of God may direct the hearts and minds of leaders and rulers to promote peace with justice.

And that the confronting power of the Spirit may see an end to inequality as resources are shared for the good of all.

Let us pray that the Spirit may inspire us to work for the fullness of God's kingdom as we say the prayer that Jesus taught us: *Our Father …*

So we look to the invigorating presence of God: Spirit of holiness, wisdom and faithfulness, wind of the Lord blowing strongly and free.

Hymn: Spirit of holiness, wisdom and faithfulness

So may the Spirit of holiness, wisdom and faithfulness bring us to fullness and freedom, pouring God's refreshing love into our hearts this day and evermore. *Amen.*

30. The God who speaks to us

21 June 2010

Good morning.

This week on Daily Service we're thinking about the God who speaks to us, the God who is himself the eternal Word bringing all things into being.

If God creates simply by virtue of what he says, that gives language the most amazing status and significance. On the one hand it ought to prompt us to be more careful about what we say to one another. On the other it should surely make us think twice in our speech to and about the God of whom glorious things are rightly to be spoken.

Hymn: Glorious things of thee are spoken

Holy God, from the treasure-store of divine speech and language you address us with your grace: help us to use our own words sparingly and with creativity, knowing that by what we say your name is praised or defamed, your will is forwarded or denied. *Amen.*

I once sat on the steps of St George's Cathedral, Cape Town trying to comfort a street-child who'd been robbed by other street-children. He had nothing and what little he had been given had been taken away from him. I tried to find the right words – which was hard because his first language was Afrikaans and mine English. Instinctively, I wanted to put an arm around him but I knew that like most street children he'd suffered so much abuse that such a gesture would probably have been misinterpreted. I had to make the point in a different way. So I dashed across the road, bought a sandwich, some orange juice and a chocolate bar, and offered him them instead.

I'd already bought myself something to eat so the two of us sat and ate together – it was a sort of alternative Eucharist on the cathedral steps whilst inside a colleague was actually breaking bread.

When the street-child came to eat his chocolate bar however he noticed that I didn't have any chocolate, so he offered me a piece. At first I was hesitant. I didn't want to deprive him. But then I took the chunk of chocolate. At which point one of the wealthiest of South Africans walked past and, recognising me, stopped to chat to both of us. He was soon being offered a piece of chocolate too. Like me, he was embarrassed and reluctant to accept it, but as he did so rich and poor were gathered together in a celebration of the Eucharist that was more real than almost any I've ever taken part in inside a church.

Reading: Mark 10: 17-27

As Jesus was setting out on a journey, a man ran up and knelt before him, and asked him, 'Good Teacher, what must I do to inherit eternal life?' Jesus said to him, 'Why do you call me good? No one is good but God alone. You know the commandments: "You shall not murder; You shall not commit adultery; You shall not steal; You shall not bear false witness; You shall not defraud; Honour your father and mother." ' He said to him, 'Teacher, I have kept all these since my youth.' Jesus, looking at him, loved him and said, 'You lack one thing; go, sell what you own, and give the money to the poor, and you will have treasure in heaven; then come, follow me.' When he heard this, he was shocked and went away grieving, for he had many possessions.

Then Jesus looked around and said to his disciples, 'How hard it will be for those who have wealth to enter the kingdom of God!' And the disciples were perplexed at these words. But Jesus said to them again, 'Children, how hard it is to enter the kingdom of God! It is easier for a camel to go through the eye of a needle than for someone who is rich to enter the kingdom of God.' They were greatly astounded and said to one another, 'Then who can be saved?' Jesus looked at them and said, 'For mortals it is impossible, but not for God; for God all things are possible.'

I've tried to set that story from Mark's Gospel in the context of a Eucharist experienced with a street-child and a billionaire because it's one of the most misinterpreted of stories. What God is saying is not that everyone with wealth must get rid of it. He directs the words to one man. This is what this man needs to do, and he needs to do it because, as his response to Jesus shows, he clings to his wealth. For me and for the rich billionaire the opposite was true. What we both had to do by way of response to God was to learn to get beyond our reluctance to receive from a street-child whom we'd boxed into the category "poor and nothing to give". Getting that chunk of chocolate to our mouths was the camel through the eye of a needle moment, God's challenge for us. What's the challenge God wants you to face today, what must you let go of and take hold of to be faithful to him and to respond to his love and mercy towards you?

Choir: I will sing of thy great mercies, Felix Mendelssohn-Bartholdy

Mendelssohn's setting of words from the psalms, I will sing of thy great mercies O Lord, taking us into our prayers.

We pray for the many challenges that the leaders of our world must address: the structural inequalities that enable some to benefit financially at the expense of others; the debt which shackles developing nations as also it depresses individuals, families and communities in our own nation, the environmental challenges to be overcome at this time in the Gulf of Mexico.

We pray for the challenges that are faced in the workplace where many are being retrenched, made redundant, or face reduced wages and longer hours.

We pray for the challenge that each one of us faces to be faithful in our calling, to be wise in our stewardship of resources, generous and loving in our concern for our neighbours.

We pray for sensitivity in what we say and do, as we seek to build the kingdom of heaven for which Jesus taught us to pray, saying: *Our Father ...*

So we look to the God who responds to all challenges through Christ's victory over sin and death. O for a thousand tongues to sing my dear Redeemer's praise.

Hymn: O for a thousand tongues

Assist us, O God, to spread abroad the good news of your saving love, as you bless us with the challenge and comfort of your abiding presence, this day and evermore. *Amen.*

31. A dream of home (return from exile)

8 July 2010

Good morning.

I'm just about to move house and job from Blackburn to London so when I saw that 'dreaming of home' was the theme for this morning – part of a week when we're thinking on the Daily Service about dreams and visions – it resonated pretty directly, since I prepared this script surrounded by packing boxes!

For Christians – as for people of other faiths too – going home – returning to God – is one of the strongest elements in our narrative tradition. Indeed, the whole Bible with its exit from Eden in Genesis and return to the new Jerusalem in Revelation is framed by this journey on which each of us has a place. Where do we feel we've reached this morning, I wonder, as we head towards that place beyond compare: Jerusalem the golden with milk and honey blest.

Hymn: Jerusalem, the golden

As we long to see your face, O Lord, as we long to feel your grace, assure us of your loving presence and bring us home. *Amen.*

"Can we go home now?" Our youngest son's plaintive request the other day when we were visiting friends really set me thinking. For of course, at three years old, his physical concept of home is about to change dramatically. The moving van will soon be outside the house and our possessions will be whisked somewhere else in God's vineyard. Of course there's emotional continuity – home in terms of his concept of family isn't changing at all. But much about our youngest son's world is about to shift for ever. Yet the question: "Can we go home now?" is not a bad place to start theologically when it comes to the business of being human. I've heard both Palestinian and Israeli families ask it when their homes have been destroyed as a consequence of conflict: "Can we go home now?" I've heard a survivor of the Holocaust – the Shoah, as Jews prefer it to be known – ask that question as dementia took a firmer grip on her mind and all she wanted was to return to her childhood home in Krakow. I've heard it asked when a Bosniak Muslim knocked on the door of the house that was her home before the conflict fifteen years ago to be greeted by a Serbian Orthodox woman wearing her dress. I can't imagine what that felt like or the two hour discussion that ensued because, though the Muslim woman desperately wanted to go home, she knew it was not likely. She had to settle for the photo albums that still lay in a trunk in the attic of her house now possessed by a stranger.

So physically, home exerts an enormous pull, especially when we are exiled from it for whatever reason. But emotionally feeling at home with ourselves, with our community, and with God, is one of the most important feelings there is. We've had more than a strong hint of it this past month as we've watched soccer's world cup dramas set against the backdrop of a South African nation continuing to rediscover the sense that it's now a home for all, a place where the sheer joy of being human belongs to everyone.

Being assured that we are loved and cherished for who we are – that others feel, that God feels at home with us, that he makes his home with us in Jesus Christ – takes us to the heart of what it means to be human.

In our reading this morning, Jeremiah's vision is of a nation reunited and celebrating its new sense of common purpose and identity.

Reading: Jeremiah 31: 1-6

At that time, says the Lord, I will be the God of all the families of Israel, and they shall be my people. Thus says the Lord: The people who survived the sword found grace in the wilderness; when Israel sought

for rest, the Lord appeared to him from far away. I have loved you
with an everlasting love; therefore I have continued my faithfulness to
you. Again I will build you, and you shall be built, O virgin Israel!
Again you shall take your tambourines, and go forth in the dance of
the merrymakers. Again you shall plant vineyards on the mountains
of Samaria; the planters shall plant, and shall enjoy the fruit. For
there shall be a day when sentinels will call in the hill country of
Ephraim: 'Come, let us go up to Zion, to the Lord our God.'

Choir: I was glad when they said unto me, Henry Purcell

Henry Purcell's setting of words from the psalms, I was glad
when they said unto me we will go into the house of the Lord, taking us into our prayers.

We pray for all who feel very far from home. For asylum seekers and refugees, for the besieged and the traumatised, for all who
are victims of circumstances beyond their control.

We remember all who are far away from their truest identity.
For those who oppress and scorn their fellow human beings. For
all whose sin estranges them from the home God seeks to make in
their hearts.

We hold before God those fleeing tyranny at this time and
those seeking to rebuild shattered lives following conflict, civil
strife and discord.

We set before ourselves that vision of the new Jerusalem to be
lived on earth as it is in heaven, as we say the prayer that Jesus
taught us: *Our Father ...*

So as we hold the vision of the kingdom before us we look to
the love of Jesus to lead us onward and homeward: O the deep,
deep love of Jesus! Vast, unmeasured, boundless, free!

Hymn: O the deep, deep love of Jesus

Lift us up to glory, O loving Lord. Lift us up to thyself. Help us to know the deep, deep love that enfolds us, surrounds us, and sustains us, as you bless us with your grace and bring us home. *Amen.*

32. Battles with our conscience

28 September 2010

Good morning.

Turn on the television any day or listen to the radio news, and you could be forgiven for thinking that conflict and outright war has become a way of life for many people in our world. This week on Daily Service we're acknowledging the place where a lot of these battles begin – which is inside each of us, as we fight to overcome our less attractive characteristics – the sins that trouble or distress others and ourselves – so that the goodness of God may shine through.

Let's offer them to God as we sing our opening hymn, All ye who seek a comfort sure in trouble and distress.

Hymn: All ye who seek a comfort sure

Bless us, O Lord, with the new grace for which we long, the new hope we follow in Jesus Christ our Lord. Bestow on us renewed hearts through the power of your love. *Amen.*

Like many Christians I love the narrative thrust of St Paul's letters, the way he constructs arguments like battles with advances and retreats – and skirmishes too – that take his readers all the while deeper into truth.

This morning we're going to hear part of Romans chapter 7, a passage in which Paul is bringing to a climax his contrast of mind and flesh, God's law and the law of sin.

Paul – a famous persecutor of Christians then one of the most conspicuous of converts to Christianity – was a person whose writings also reveal immense inner conflict. A Jew who believed that God's covenant with his people stood for ever, yet a man who sensed that life in the Spirit – the gift which is Jesus Christ – was not just for the Jewish community, but for everyone. He didn't always seem to know how to hold it all together.

So let's wrestle with this famous passage from chapter 7.

Reading: Romans 7: 14-25a

For we know that the law is spiritual; but I am of the flesh, sold into slavery under sin. I do not understand my own actions. For I do not do what I want, but I do the very thing I hate. Now if I do what I do not want, I agree that the law is good. But in fact it is no longer I that do it, but sin that dwells within me. For I know that nothing good dwells within me, that is, in my flesh. I can will what is right, but I cannot do it. For I do not do the good I want, but the evil I do not want is what I do. Now if I do what I do not want, it is no longer I that do it, but sin that dwells within me.

So I find it to be a law that when I want to do what is good, evil lies close at hand. For I delight in the law of God in my inmost self, but I see in my members another law at war with the law of my mind, making me captive to the law of sin that dwells in my members. Wretched man that I am! Who will rescue me from this body of death? Thanks be to God through Jesus Christ our Lord!

A few days ago I sat in a bus shelter outside John Keble Church in North London where I've recently moved as vicar whilst a poor disconsolate bundle of humanity poured out his soul to me. "I hadn't meant to do it," he said. "I didn't understand my actions. I did the very thing I didn't want to do," he added." I lost my wife and my kids. I knew I was wrong. I know what goodness is," he continued. "It was as if something took over … evil … oh, I'm such a fool … who on earth can help me now?"

How similar his tale was to the passage from Romans chapter 7 we heard. And which of us hasn't been there or at least been close. But as I held the gentleman's hand and he sobbed and asked me to say the Lord's Prayer with him I hope he sensed the presence of Christ transforming his sin and healing his misery through the power of redeeming love.

Choir: Expectans expectavi, Charles Wood

Charles Wood's setting of words by Charles Hamilton Sorley, a young poet killed in the First World War, 'This sanctuary of my soul I keep white and whole ... unlatched, and lit, if thou shouldst care to enter.'

And so, making room in our hearts for the love of God, we pray for those whose inner conflict lands them on the wrong side of the tracks; for all estranged from their love ones as a result of wrong-doing and sin.

For all who do not know the way back to God's love and cannot sense the divine presence rushing out to meet them and bring them home.

For all whose sinfulness is compounded by circumstances beyond their control.

That each may know the power of Christ crucified, the well-spring of salvation for all.

We pray for all called to positions of leadership that their wrestling with conscience may promote peace, stability and the common good.

And we pray for ourselves, that in our moments of temptation or vulnerability we may know the strength of God's kingdom for which Jesus taught us to pray, saying: *Our Father ...*

O God, who wouldest fold both heaven and earth in a single peace: let the design of thy great love lighten upon the waste of our wraths and sorrows: and give peace to thy Church, peace among nations, peace in our dwellings, and peace in our hearts; through thy Son, our Saviour Jesus Christ. *Amen.*

Eric Milner-White

So may we never feel discouraged or think our spiritual wrestlings are in vain but seek the balm in Gilead.

Choir: There is a balm in Gilead, to make the wounded whole

May we know the balm in Gilead that makes the wounded whole, the balm in Gilead that heals the sin-sick soul, and may God bless us with his love and grace, this day and evermore. *Amen.*

33. A visionary preacher: Ezekiel

3 November 2010

Good morning.

This week because it's All Saintstide, Daily Service is focusing on heroes and heroines of the faith.

Today, we recall from the Hebrew Bible Ezekiel a figure from the time when the Jewish people were exiled in Babylon.

We know almost nothing about him – he's only mentioned twice in the book that bears his name – but he's a hero because when he looked at the exile – the valley of dry bones as he put it – he saw beyond the no hope way God's people had got themselves there. He knew they could live again and what he put into words has captured the imagination whether for Raphael in paint or for Mahler in music.

It's part of that rich treasure store, the wondrous tale, as our first hymn puts it, the hand of God no less, guiding God's flock from age to age.

Hymn: Thy hand, O God, has guided

Guide us with your right hand, O Lord. Help us to live by the power and victory of your glorious resurrection. *Amen.*

I've recently returned from a trip to Cape Town in South Africa, where I worked for some years, and where, as ever, I've been struck by the stories of hope and resurrection you literally bump into. A street child who'd become an undergraduate engineer at the University of Cape Town – an amazing transformation by any standards. And another student at the university who lives in drug- and gang-ridden Manenberg but whose laughter and energy are making him a positive force for good.

But it was sitting watching Western Province play Rugby – for once this wasn't a valley of dry bones as they won the match – that I had the great privilege of meeting Leon and Lorna Levy.

Leon was one of the treason trialists with Nelson Mandela in the 1960s – acquitted but sent into a thirty-four year exile to the UK – along with his wife Lorna who became a local London councilor and a leading anti-apartheid activist.

People with a real-life story of the valley of dry bones. People, like Ezekiel, who know what it's like to be exiled from their homeland, and what it is to live with that haunting question: "Can these dry bones live?" but who answer it themselves by holding on to and working for a vision of change and renewal when all the signs around them suggest that this is never going to happen.

Reading: Ezekiel 37: 1-6, 11-14

The hand of the Lord came upon me, and he brought me out by the spirit of the Lord and set me down in the middle of a valley; it was full of bones. He led me all round them; there were very many lying in the valley, and they were very dry. He said to me, 'Mortal, can these bones live?' I answered, 'O Lord God, you know.' Then he said to me, 'Prophesy to these bones, and say to them: O dry bones, hear the word of the Lord. Thus says the Lord God to these bones: I will cause breath to enter you, and you shall live. I will lay sinews on you, and will cause flesh to come upon you, and cover you with skin, and put breath in you, and you shall live; and you shall know that I am the Lord.'

Then he said to me, 'Mortal, these bones are the whole house of Israel. They say, "Our bones are dried up, and our hope is lost; we are cut off completely." Therefore prophesy, and say to them, Thus says the Lord God: I am going to open your graves, and bring you up from your graves, O my people; and I will bring you back to the land of Israel. And you shall know that I am the Lord, when I open your graves, and bring you up from your graves, O my people. I will put my spirit within you, and you shall live, and I will place you on your own soil; then you shall know that I, the Lord, have spoken and will act, says the Lord.'

People renewed, resurrected, returned to the land of their ancestors. For Leon and Lorna Levy this happened when Leon's fellow trialist, Nelson Mandela, became president of a democratic South Africa and they came home. But returning from exile is never easy as they'd testify, especially when the values for which people fought – and made such sacrifices – seem subverted by the materialism of a new elite, and you begin to feel an exile all over again; certainly that you've begun another long journey to the fullness of freedom.

Choir: O taste and see, Ralph Vaughan Williams

Vaughan Williams' setting of words from the Psalms, O taste and see, and leading us into our prayers.

Let us pray for all who hold onto a vision of change and renewal amidst the most difficult of circumstances.

For the millions in South Africa whose lives are still blighted by poverty, lack of health care or educational opportunity.

For our sisters and brothers in Zimbabwe shackled by oppression, overwhelmed by natural disaster in Pakistan and for people of all faiths and ethnicities in the Holy Land, imprisoned by suspicion, fear and conflict.

For all in our own community who lack material resource and access to care.

For those most affected by cut-backs in service provision, or who feel disenfranchised by the decisions of political leaders.

A prayer based on words of Sir Francis Drake:

O Lord God, when you give to your servants to endeavour any great matter, grant us also to know that it is not the beginning, but the continuing of the same unto the end, until it be thoroughly finished, which yields the true glory; through him, who for the finishing of your work laid down his life, our Redeemer, Jesus Christ. *Amen.*

As we look for support in our search for renewal, justice and resurrection, may we know the fullness of God's kingdom praying the words that Jesus taught us: *Our Father ...*

So let us pray that the light of resurrection may dawn in all its fullness, as we acknowledge its source: Immortal, invisible, God only-wise.

Hymn: Immortal, invisible

So may the light of the resurrection renew us with divine grace this day and evermore. *Amen.*

34. Healing wounded lives (World AIDS Day)

1 December 2010

Good morning.

Today, worldwide, we remember those living with HIV and AIDS. It's a day which inevitably raises difficult questions about the nature of human living and especially the meaning of suffering. It's a day when the sheer scale of the millions who live with the HIV virus and have died as a result of AIDS threatens to overwhelm us. So it's a day to focus down, to think of the one person whose story we know, and who, as our brother or sister, each of us is called to serve.

Hymn: Brother, sister, let me serve you

Pray, Lord, that we may have the grace to be as Christ to friend and stranger, to hold out a hand to those needing support, to light a candle for all in darkness, to share one another's joys and sorrows, until we've seen this journey through. *Amen.*

Few of us who were present at the 13th International AIDS Conference in Durban South Africa in the year 2000, will surely ever forget the speech given by a little eleven year old South African boy, born with HIV, Nkosi Johnson.

In his young life not only had he suffered great pain and sickness, he'd also been ostracised when he attempted to assert his God-given right to education, and found that parents at his Johannesburg school didn't want their sons or daughters educated alongside someone living with HIV.

With a calm insightfulness way beyond his years he had him-self helped them to understand that he could harm no-one and that like everyone else he had unique gifts to share. Somehow he'd turned that unpromising experience of prejudice right round, and, speaking for everyone living with HIV and AIDS, he ended his speech with words that touched millions.

"Care for us and accept us" he said, "we are all human beings. We are normal. We have hands. We have feet. We can walk, we can talk, we have needs just like everyone else – don't be afraid of us – we are all the same!"

It was a vision of a common humanity to unite all of us, HIV positive or negative, a vision of acceptance and hope very close to the words we hear now from the final chapter of the book of Reve-lation.

Reading: Revelation 22: 1-7

Then the angel showed me the river of the water of life, bright as crys-tal, flowing from the throne of God and of the Lamb through the middle of the street of the city. On either side of the river is the tree of life with its twelve kinds of fruit, producing its fruit each month; and the leaves of the tree are for the healing of the nations. Nothing ac-cursed will be found there any more. But the throne of God and of the Lamb will be in it, and his servants will worship him; they will see his face, and his name will be on their foreheads. And there will be no more night; they need no light of lamp or sun, for the Lord God will be their light, and they will reign for ever and ever.

Few visions are more beautiful and inspiring than the streams of water flowing through the city as bright as crystal and giving life to the trees from whose fruit and leaves, healing is to abound. But the danger with such a heaven-bound vision is that it can sometimes be of little earthly use.

I remember stopping some well-meaning but wrong-headed

143

cleric at an AIDS Conference once when he'd launched into flights of biblical fancy about how we needed to prevent prejudice against those with HIV and AIDS, and what their care needs were in general. "They're sitting right in front of you, Father," I said. "Don't lecture them, ask them!"

He did and it changed the whole conference. Since the truth that Nkosi Johnson and thousands of others like him have sought to embody and advance is that only when those living with HIV and AIDS are given control of the pandemic – are put up front to show that they're just like everyone else and capable of sorting and sourcing their own care – will perceptions and prejudices shift.

This means focusing on what's become known as the principle of decent care, which transcends old-fashioned do-gooding for the needy by thoroughly patient-centred practice.

I'm thinking here of a clinic I know in rural South Africa, for instance, run by those living with HIV and AIDS themselves, where they've taught local leaders not to build western-style individual homes which isolate people and make care networks difficult, but to cluster homes in a traditional African way that makes care feasible in a community where everyone is affected and almost everyone infected with HIV and AIDS. It's such a simple idea but it's broken down stigma and prejudice, and it's allowed those streams of healing water to flow.

Choir: The Lord's my shepherd, Bob Chilcott

Bob Chilcott's setting of the twenty third psalm, The Lord's my shepherd, leading us into our prayers.

We pray for all who are living with HIV and AIDS that they may know their place in God's heart and the support of their neighbours in their quest for treatment, acceptance and respect.

We remember all who today will pass through death's dark vale. May they be anointed by the comforting presence of God and know their place at the heavenly banquet.

We ask for grace to enter more deeply the joys and sorrows of our fellow human beings, and to face the challenges about ourselves that such engagement risks.

We entrust into the hands of God all with specialist skills to address the pandemic in body, mind and spirit.

We celebrate the positive and life-changing contributions of those living with HIV and AIDS. May we always treasure the enrichment that they bring.

We pray that all ignorance and prejudice may be redirected into compassion and respect for a common humanity.

We give thanks to God for the opportunities to participate in the healing and wholeness of his promised kingdom, for which we long when we pray the words that Jesus taught us: *Our Father …*

So we acknowledge that God's kingdom comes through the brokenness of our humanity: Earth's fragile beauties we possess as pilgrim gifts from God.

Hymn: Earth's fragile beauties

May the wounded heart of love, tainted by human hatred and spite, and bearing our sins and sorrows, bring healing and hope to all God's children as it restores in each of us the divine image, this day and evermore. *Amen.*

35. Light in the darkness

14 December 2010

Good morning.

When the earliest Christians wanted to describe the light of Jesus impacting on the life of cities and towns around the Holy Land and beyond, they used the picture of the thief coming in the night. It's a strange image in many ways. Since being burgled is an affronting, disruptive and indeed invasive experience, one that turns our lives upside down. But it's that 'upside-downess' that they wanted to capture, so that startled at the solemn warning and dazzled by the light of a new reality people would respond to the urgent cry: Hark, a herald voice is calling, Christ is nigh it seems to say.

Hymn: Hark a herald voice is calling

As you startle us with the brightness of your presence, Lord, come into our hearts to cast away the dreams of darkness and help us to live as children of the day. *Amen.*

Once, when I was teaching and living at a girls boarding school, I sank gratefully into my bed one night, only to be startled forty-five minutes later by the sound of voices and what I thought must be the rustling of paper in my study opposite. As I was very sleepy I didn't react too quickly and before I knew it two figures were standing at the foot of my bed. Sitting bolt upright I some-how stammered out a sentence that is among the most ridiculous I have ever uttered: 'Excuse me, how may I help you!' But polite-ness obviously paid off as the two intruders swiftly fled down the stairs, out through the bathroom, and onto the roof of the neigh-bouring boarding house.

Jolted from my sleepiness I also sped down the stairs but too late to catch them – a job which the Cheltenham Constabulary undertook most nobly!

Returning to my study, I found a depressing scene with books and papers scattered all over the place. But then, amid the chaos, I saw a photograph I had mislaid – the only photograph I possess of my maternal grandfather who died long before my birth. I guess that I must have used it as a bookmark and that it was unknowingly unearthed by the intruders.

Amidst my irritation and the chaos before me it was a moment of revelation, exactly the sort of moment that Paul wanted the church in Thessalonica to experience, when he wrote them these words.

Reading: 1 Thessalonians 5: 2-11

For you yourselves know very well that the day of the Lord will come like a thief in the night. When they say, 'There is peace and security', then sudden destruction will come upon them, as labour pains come upon a pregnant woman, and there will be no escape! But you, beloved, are not in darkness, for that day to surprise you like a thief; for you are all children of light and children of the day; we are not of the night or of darkness. So then, let us not fall asleep as others do, but let us keep awake and be sober; for those who sleep sleep at night, and those who are drunk get drunk at night. But since we belong to the day, let us be sober, and put on the breastplate of faith and love, and for a helmet the hope of salvation. For God has destined us not for wrath but for obtaining salvation through our Lord Jesus Christ, who died for us, so that whether we are awake or asleep we may live with him. Therefore encourage one another and build up each other, as indeed you are doing.

Those words from the very first Christian document to have survived give us a sense both of the impact of the light of Christ in his times and the expected urgency of his return. He would come like a thief in the night. And though burglary is an immensely painful and invasive experience it can, as I discovered, have both its lighter and deeper sides. The two lads at the foot of my bed were very disappointed to be greeted by a male voice. It wasn't quite what they expected. At least that's what I was told! But neither did I expect to discover the photograph I'd supposed that I'd lost. And it's that, the long-lost image and imprint of the divine in us, that we are meant to discover as we journey through the Advent season by the light of a lone star towards the one who is the light of everything. We don't discover it easily of course. We find it precisely where we don't perhaps expect it, amidst the mess and debris which is the world we inhabit. Which is a thought, perhaps, to tease even the sleepiest of us into the light of day.

Choir: Light of the world, John Dankworth

John Dankworth's setting of words by Paul Wigmore, Light of the World, leading us into our prayers.

We pray that God will reveal to us the light beyond shadow, the joy beyond tears, the love that is greater than our darkest fears.

We pray especially for those who live in the darkness and debris of conflict, and for all whose darkness is an inner reality, overwhelming them with a sense of guilt, or sin or shame.

We remember the many people who seek to bring light to others. Carers who bring calm amidst the confusion of illness, friends who lend a hand and speak a word of comfort amidst the ups and downs of life.

We recall ourselves to the presence of Jesus, the one who promises comfort but also challenge.

We trust in Christ's ability to restore the lost image of the divine in each of us as we pray for the fullness of his kingdom in the words that he taught us: *Our Father ...*

Choir: Cast thy burden upon the Lord, Felix Mendelssohn-Bartholdy

So we look to Jesus as Saviour of all: Creator of the stars of night, thy people's everlasting light.

Hymn: Creator of the stars of night

Come Lord, creator of the stars of night, set us free and bless us now with the brightness of your glory, this day and evermore. *Amen.*

36. Holocaust Memorial Day

27 January 2011

Good morning.

One of the most powerful experiences of my ministry as a priest was the night when I joined a mother and father soon after they'd received the news that their teenaged son had died whilst out with his friends. They were shocked, devastated, utterly bewildered. There was nothing to say. I just held their hands. It was literally too awful for words. Suddenly the mother sprinted down the stairs of their second-floor flat and was heading towards the cathedral next door. I knew it was shut so I ran after her. But as she reached the entrance so I stopped transfixed by the visceral nature of what she did next. For she was standing, banging on the door shouting, "Why, God? Why. Why, oh why?" Shaking a fist at God – like Job; wrestling with God – like Jacob; she was articulating the question that must be close to the lips of all conscious of it on a day like this, the sixty-sixth anniversary of the liberation of the Auschwitz death camp, why in God's name did the Holocaust, the Shoah, the annihilation, as the Jewish community refers to it, happen?

Music: Psalm 130

A prayer scratched by a Jewish prisoner on a cell wall in Cologne during the Shoah

I believe in the sun even when I cannot see it.
I believe in love even when I cannot feel it.
I believe in God even when he is silent.

I've always found that prayer – and many like it to emerge from within the horrors of the death camps – inspiring. In a characteristically Jewish way, like psalm 130, which we heard a few moments ago, it both laments and praises. It asserts God's seeming absence and yet his abiding presence.

Elie Wiesel, the Auschwitz survivor, recalls the afternoon that the Jews spent putting God on trial in the camp and finding God guilty for doing nothing to stop the suffering, after which the rabbi who had pronounced the verdict stood up and said, "Now, gentleman, we say the Shabbat prayers." On the one hand this, on the other hand this – both frankly seeming to contradict one another.

It's a tension with which all of us live. The woman who bangs on the door in anger at God one day is the same woman who irons the altar linen the next. The man I travelled with the other day in tears on the way to his wife's funeral yet laughing and smiling to try and calm his screaming grandchild at the same time.

Of course in relation to the Holocaust it's a tension that people have tried to resolve one way or another. The Jewish theologian Bernard Maza said it was the Jews fault – God's fury was poured out on them because they weren't Jewish enough. That shocked a lot of people, not least many Christians who knew that their long history of anti-Judaism, emanating from the blame attached to the Jewish people for the death of Christ in the Gospels, had more to do with the ovens of Auschwitz than did God. Another Jewish theologian, Richard Rubenstein said that God was now dead. He must be since he was too useless to be believed in; though later Rubenstein relented and brought God back into his thinking, and also maybe his praying. Eliezar Berkovits, said God wasn't dead or angry but hidden. Ignaz Maybaum, saw the Shoah as a necessary sacrifice, part of the divine plan for the world to bring it back to God. But others thought that frankly a bit extreme. I put all this to Rabbi Lionel Blue the other day when I was chatting to him. He said, "What do you expect. Ask four Rabbis and you'll get at least six opinions!" But we agreed that another Jewish theologian, Emil Fackenheim, had much going for him, since he didn't really attempt to explain why it had happened – which human being can really answer that question? – but suggested instead that our task now as Jews, Christians, people of all faiths and world views, is to mend the world. It's perhaps this hope to which the Book of the Lamentations chapter three points as it explores much of the same confused terrain.

Reading: Lamentations 3: 1-6, 19-24

I am one who has seen affliction under the rod of God's wrath; he has driven and brought me into darkness without any light; against me alone he turns his hand, again and again, all day long. He has made my flesh and my skin waste away, and broken my bones; he has besieged and enveloped me with bitterness and tribulation; he has made me sit in darkness like the dead of long ago. The thought of my affliction and my homelessness is wormwood and gall! My soul continually thinks of it and is bowed down within me. But this I call to mind, and therefore I have hope:

The steadfast love of the Lord never ceases, his mercies never come to an end; they are new every morning; great is your faithfulness. 'The Lord is my portion,' says my soul,' therefore I will hope in him.'

But perhaps hope is too much for a day like this. And what we have to settle for instead is not that rush to make things better – even mending the world can frankly wait for a day or two – or the terrible forced smiliness, the instinct that some Christians have within their theology to see everything so surely in the light of resurrection that they avoid the costliness of the cross altogether – no, what we have to settle for today are the two m's: memory and mercy. Memory of a horror beyond our understanding yet within our capability – perhaps each of us could have stoked those ovens given the wrong set of circumstances – and divine mercy through which we plead for a world where such disorder lurks in us.

Music: Kyrie from Mass in B Minor, Johann Sebastian Bach

The Kyrie from Bach's Mass in B minor, taking us into our prayers

We pray for all those for whom this day continues to reawaken memories of terrible violence, suffering and dehumanization, especially remembering our Christian complicity in this.

We remember the survivors of the Shoah, often so guilty that they have enjoyed the gift of life when their families and loved ones perished.

We give thanks for the witness of those able to speak about their experiences, for the work of the Holocaust Memorial Day Trust, as also we remember all whose greatest gift to humanity has been simply to live, to build family and community once again.

We pray for the work of those agencies which have done so much to prevent genocide, as also we pray for all survivors of the genocides of our own times.

As we seek understanding so we pray for grace to remember the past in order to re-member and build anew the world of peace and justice for which Jesus prayed: *Our Father …*

So, seeking deliverance from evil, and a world where peace flourishes, we pray that this journey will begin as we draw close to one another with respect and reverence.

Music: O brother man, fold to thy heart thy brother

Bless us O Lord, that amidst the ashes of all that's worst in human experience you may plant in us the tree of peace and hope, this day and evermore. *Amen.*

37. God and the scientist

24 February 2011

Good morning

This week on Daily Service we're thinking about different sorts of people with whom God speaks, and today we consider the relationship between God and the scientist.

It's axiomatic of course for people of faith that God creates, indeed that God is responsible for the whole universe. Which is the point in any pub conversation where things usually fall apart, someone invariably mentioning science and the seeming incompatibility of what religious folk believe and what scientists say. But science and faith need not be opponents, they can and ought to be sisters, sisters with different yet complimentary perspectives, both able, to give praise to the Lord, the almighty, the king of creation.

Hymn: Praise to the Lord

Praising you, Lord, for the glory of creation, may we delight as much in the beautiful patterns that scientists see at the heart of all matter, as in the visible beauty of the first snowdrops of late winter. *Amen.*

When I was on the staff of Westminster Abbey I once gave a tour of the building to a group clearly composed of rather fundamentalist creationists. I ended it, perhaps somewhat naughtily, by taking them to the grave of Charles Darwin.

I wish I could put into words the shocked look on their faces, as I waxed lyrical about the glories of evolution, the connected insights of science and faith, and the courage of the Dean of Westminster who'd buried Darwin in a place over which all the royals and VIPs would have to walk.

But behind the somewhat confronting nature of this moment, was the conviction I learned as a teenager from one of the most remarkable priests of recent times that not only do science and religion ask complimentary questions – science deals with the how of things, religion with the why of them – but that both are in fact concerned to discern the patterning and beauty, at the heart of the cosmos.

As a sixteen year old, when I first encountered John Polkinghorne – then a curate in Bristol but previously a professor of particle physics at Cambridge University – my chief concern was to play the organ for him!

But as I got to know him a little better so I began to understand that the exquisite patterning of the quarks – some of the smallest particles there are – that he'd helped to discover in his work, spilled over into an enthusiasm – a passion no less – to discern the creative and redemptive orderliness and beauty in everything. All was of a piece. I would attempt to play Bach and as we chatted about how it reflected the God who orders and reorders, who creates and redeems, so he would teach me the majesty of the maths and physics I struggled to master at school but for which he gave me so much respect because he showed something of the art and beauty in it, the majesty no less about which our reading from Isaiah speaks so eloquently.

Reading: Isaiah 40: 18-28

To whom then will you liken God, or what likeness compare with him? An idol? - A workman casts it, and a goldsmith overlays it with gold, and casts for it silver chains.

As a gift one chooses mulberry wood – wood that will not rot – then seeks out a skilled artisan to set up an image that will not topple.

Have you not known? Have you not heard? Has it not been told you from the beginning? Have you not understood from the foundations of the earth? It is he who sits above the circle of the earth, and its inhabitants are like grasshoppers; who stretches out the heavens like a curtain, and spreads them like a tent to live in; who brings princes to naught, and makes the rulers of the earth as nothing.

*Scarcely are they planted, scarcely sown, scarcely has their stem
taken root in the earth, when he blows upon them, and they wither,
and the tempest carries them off like stubble.*

*To whom then will you compare me, or who is my equal? says the
Holy One. Lift up your eyes on high and see: Who created these? He
who brings out their host and numbers them, calling them all by
name; because he is great in strength, mighty in power, not one is
missing.*

*Why do you say, O Jacob, and speak, O Israel, 'My way is hidden
from the Lord, and my right is disregarded by my God'? Have you not
known? Have you not heard? The Lord is the everlasting God, the
Creator of the ends of the earth. He does not faint or grow weary; his
understanding is unsearchable.*

Unsearchable, yes, in the sense that neither the theologian or
the scientist may ever grasp the fullness of reality, its nature or
purpose. But not literally unsearchable. For whether 'faith seeking
understanding' as for Anselm, or 'matter seeking explication' as
for Polkinghorne, both are caught up in the great conversation not
just between God and the scientist but God and the whole of humanity, a conversation that needs to face the other side of the coin
too. Since beyond the beautiful patterning of creation is the dark
side, the disorder – a necessary reality as Polkinghorne would
argue both scientifically and in religious terms – which sees tec-
tonic plates move in such a way as to allow for the earth's
resources nutritionally to be replenished – all life is reliant on this
– but which also causes the spire of Christchurch Cathedral in
New Zealand to collapse and many to die in an earthquake. This is
not easy stuff. It requires all the resources of head and
understanding, heart and thinking we can muster.

Choir: God be in my head, John Rutter

156

John Rutter's setting of words from the Sarum Primer, God be in my head, taking us into our prayers.

Acknowledging that there is so much we don't know or understand about God's world, let us give thanks to God for the attention of scientist and believer alike to the intricacy, the beauty, the patterning – and the necessary disorder – at the heart of creation.

Let us pray for an end to the stand-off which so often seems to exist in public debate where reason and revelation are set against one another rather than seen as necessary neighbours and friends.

Let us remember all who wrestle with the issues in contexts of great human suffering, especially at this time for people of Christchurch, New Zealand, for those who have lost love ones or livelihoods, homes or hope, that they may be sustained in their hour of need.

Let us remember all scientists and theologians who face difficult ethical decisions in some of the most sensitive areas of life, especially in the field of genetics.

In the face of so much human turmoil and disorder in the world – in Egypt, in Libya, in Bahrain and Tunisia – let us pray that energised by the insights of science and faith we may use our gifts to discern God's will for humanity.

So let us pray for the coming of the kingdom, in the words that Jesus Christ taught us: *Our Father ...*

As we pray for the kingdom so we see signs of it in the beauty of creation and redemption: Lord of beauty thine the splendour shewn in earth and sky and sea.

Hymn: Lord of beauty

Lord of beauty, guide our footsteps into all truth, as you bless us with a vision of your unending love, this day and evermore. *Amen.*

38. The light of God's presence

30 March 2011

Choir: Thy word is a lantern, Ian Tracey

Good morning.

There's an old saying that runs 'it's better to light a candle than to curse the darkness.' in other words when things get tough what's needed is a small dose of reality to get our feet back on track. But sometimes, as the well-known words of our opening hymn suggest, the reverse is the problem: there's so much light we shield ourselves from it. Immortal, invisible, God only-wise.

Hymn: Immortal, invisible

When the splendour of light blinds us, Lord, or when light seems hidden from our eyes, show us the reality of your abiding presence. *Amen.*

Our music this morning is using light as a metaphor for our sense of God's presence in the world, for the way in which we bathe or hide ourselves in divine light so that God is acknowledged or shut out.

To explore this idea, we're about to hear a passage of scripture from the Book of Numbers, involving a talking donkey. But as the transition from candles to donkeys isn't an easy one, we need some context.

Balak, king of Moab is fearful that the Israelites, following a victory over the Amorites, are going to turn to what's left of his kingdom. So he does what kings do in the ancient world which is to hire a mercenary diviner – a seer – from Syria who's famous for his blessings and curses. Balak basically wants this seer, Balaam, to curse Israel. But faithful Balaam consults God and rebuffs Balak's request. Which is where we come to this morning's section of Numbers chapter 22 and a God who, surprisingly, is now roused to anger against the very person, Balaam, who's not shutting him out but actually about to do his will.

Reading: Numbers 22: 27-35

God's anger was kindled because Balaam was going, and the angel of the Lord took his stand in the road as his adversary. When the donkey saw the angel of the Lord, it lay down under Balaam; and Balaam's anger was kindled, and he struck the donkey with his staff. Then the Lord opened the mouth of the donkey, and it said to Balaam, 'What have I done to you, that you have struck me these three times?' Balaam said to the donkey, 'Because you have made a fool of me! I wish I had a sword in my hand! I would kill you right now!' But the donkey said to Balaam, 'Am I not your donkey, which you have ridden all your life to this day? Have I been in the habit of treating you in this way?' And he said, 'No.'

Then the Lord opened the eyes of Balaam, and he saw the angel of the Lord standing in the road, with his drawn sword in his hand; and he bowed down, falling on his face. The angel of the Lord said to him, 'Why have you struck your donkey these three times? I have come out as an adversary, because your way is perverse before me. The donkey saw me, and turned away from me these three times. If it had not turned away from me, surely I would by now have killed you and let it live.' Then Balaam said to the angel of the Lord, 'I have sinned, for I did not know that you were standing in the road to oppose me. Now therefore, if it is displeasing to you, I will return home.' The angel of the Lord said to Balaam, 'Go with the men; but speak only what I tell you to speak.' So Balaam went on with the officials of Balak.

It's hard to account for the bizarre nature of this passage in any other way than that it's what scholars call an interpolation. In other words it was added later, perhaps from a different tradition that held Balaam to be unfaithful to God. So he gets tested by a speaking donkey who makes sure that he isn't shutting God out or avoiding the task God has entrusted to him.

In the context of Shrek the movie, a wise-speaking donkey makes perfect sense. In the book of Numbers it's less realistic perhaps. But the point is the same, to open eyes to the wisdom that arrests us by blocking our path on the road, the wisdom we may literally trip over if we have eyes to see, in other words the light we find beyond shadow.

Choir: Light beyond shadow, John Dankworth

Light beyond shadow, the words by Paul Wigmore, to the music of John Dankworth, and taking us into our prayers.

We pray for all who like Balaam seem to be following God's way but who may in reality use religion as a means to shut God out by hiding behind custom and tradition that masks less than worthy desires or aspirations. We pray for all who shut God out of their lives, through the wilfulness of sin or who feel shut off from God by the complexity of their circumstances.

We remember especially all who resort to violence in the name of religion, in the Middle East, in Libya and in Pakistan, that wisdom may confront them on the pathway they may be taking to destruction.

We express penitence for those ways in which we are blinded to divine truth in our own lives and pray that the season of Lent will be a time for eyes to be opened to the Christ who renews and redeems.

A Prayer of Rabindranath Tagore:

When the heart is hard and parched up,
Come upon me with a shower of mercy.
When grace is lost from life, come with a burst of song.
When tumultuous work raises its din on all sides shutting me
out from beyond, come to me, my Lord of silence, with thy peace
and rest.
When my beggarly heart sits crouched, shut up in a corner,
break open the door, my king, and come with the ceremony of a
king.
When desire blinds the mind with delusion and dust, O thou
holy One, thou wakeful, come with thy light and thy thunder.

So we pray that the light of the kingdom may dawn in our
hearts as we say together: *Our Father ...*

We look to the light of God, too bright for our eyes yet shining
in our humanity in Jesus Christ, as we sing the hymn, Can man by
searching find out God or formulate his ways?

Hymn: Can man by searching find out God or formulate his ways?

As we recognise divine light in the one who breaks into our
world and makes his glory known, who speaks to us in the person
of Jesus Christ, and invites us to live together in the light of his
presence, we pray his blessing upon us this day and evermore.
Amen.

39. Fatherly love

1 June 2011

Good morning.

"D'you not celebrate father's day at your church?" a man shouted to me the other day. "I didn't see it on your notice-board," he continued. "You have Mothering Sunday don't you?"

It was the start of a long but fruitful discussion on how the church does or does not celebrate love, especially that awesome calling to model love as a parent in which so many share, and which comes from the one whose goodness never fails, who gives us all we lack: the king of love.

Hymn: The king of love my shepherd is

King of love, whose goodness never fails, as we sing your praise may we learn more the truth of your costly love which transforms and saves. *Amen.*

The failure of the churches to embrace father's day and to do the traditional thing with a secular celebration – which is of course to Christianise it – is in many ways very surprising. Not least the loving relationship of father and son is axiomatic for Christian belief. Without it, no incarnation, no God become human, no salvation, no son challenging then doing the will of the father. In short, no Gospel to speak of at all.

Perhaps there's a fear that if we focus on fathers and sons in an earthly sense we'll somehow lose the divine mystery of the love of God in Christ.

But belief has to start with what we know – not with what we don't! We have to move out from human experience towards the edge of mystery if we're to orientate ourselves at all. And as the father of three sons under the age of twelve what my relationship with them teaches me about the nature of love is quite simply the raw data that points me to the divine nature of love.

At the moment, they're all at ages where they are pushing boundaries. And I'm needing to know when to hold on, what to hold on to, and when to let go.

Words of the poet Cecil Day Lewis, written as he watches his son Daniel running away from him amidst a scatter of boys on the first day of school as he feels a sense of parting that gnaws at him, and realises 'How self-hood begins with a walking away and love is proved in the letting go.'

Lewis asserts that this is what God perfectly shows in Jesus Christ. The very maternal language of our reading from John chapter 17 says much the same.

Reading: John 17: 20-26

'I ask not only on behalf of these, but also on behalf of those who will believe in me through their word, that they may all be one. As you, Father, are in me and I am in you, may they also be in us, so that the world may believe that you have sent me. The glory that you have given me I have given them, so that they may be one, as we are one, I in them and you in me, that they may become completely one, so that the world may know that you have sent me and have loved them even as you have loved me. Father, I desire that those also, whom you have given me, may be with me where I am, to see my glory, which you have given me because you loved me before the foundation of the world.

'Righteous Father, the world does not know you, but I know you; and these know that you have sent me. I made your name known to them, and I will make it known, so that the love with which you have loved me may be in them, and I in them.'

On first hearing, all that 'I in you' and 'you in me' language – language that suggests the intimacy of child in a mother's womb – is quite confusing with everyone intrinsically connected to everyone else. But when the gaps are exposed – the fact that the mutual love of father and son which keeps them distinct yet makes them one isn't shared by everyone – we perhaps begin to see that these gaps in understanding or connectedness could be the god-shaped spaces into which our own attempts at loving may be offered. Loving that'll be costly for sure but which is still the only way humans may grow and may know the God we see in Jesus Christ.

Choir: Thy perfect love, John Rutter

Thy perfect love. Fifteenth century words to the music of John Rutter, and taking us into our prayers.

We pray for an ability to cherish and honour the parental love – in its many forms – by which we learn what love itself is, as we also remember those for whom their relationship with their parents is a difficult and challenging reality.

We pray for grace to nurture the spark of love wherever we see it, love for God, love for neighbour, love which promotes that self-respect on which all relationships depend.

We pray for faithfulness to work at our loving, to be generous about the faults we see in others, and rigorous in overcoming aspects of our own nature which are less than attractive.

We remember at this time all with responsibility for the elderly, the infirm, and the frail, that they may show respect and love for all in their care.

We pray for the imagination to see in our feeble attempts at loving and being loved the God who is perfect love, and who has taught us to call him abba, father, as we say together his Son's prayer: Our Father ...

So we look to the love perfected in Christ and to be completed in us: Love divine, all love's excelling.

Hymn: Love divine

Lost in wonder, love and praise may we know your blessing upon us O Lord, upon us this day and evermore. Amen.

40. Answering terror and violence

7 July 2011

Choir: We will lay our burden down, arranged John Bell

Good morning.

I'm by nurture – and I hope by nature – a good morning person. Long ago my parents taught me to wish people a good morning. It's a habit I'd find hard to break. It's actually – if you think about it – a habit of holiness – directing people to God's morning, his gift of a new day that's more important than one supposes. But some days those two words do stick in the gullet.

We cannot help but recall the events of this day, the seventh of July, in 2005, the day for Londoners that changed the landscape of our nation, indeed our world.

Was it a good morning? No, at one level, of course not. It was horrible. But for all its horrors it was nonetheless God's morning, dawning like that Friday long ago, which we still call Good Friday, a day on which we learn God's presence amidst not beyond the horrors of life, a day on which we pray, Thy kingdom come, O God, thy rule, O Christ, begin.

Hymn: Thy kingdom come, O God

Arise, O morning star, never set though the darkness engulfs our hearts. Arise, and make known your kingdom of peace, this day and always. *Amen.*

This week I've been hosting an American friend, the former marine Rye Barcott, who knows better than most what it means to discern peace on the way to war in Afghanistan and Iraq, conflicts directly related to the awfulness of a 7/7.

Barcott's is a remarkable story. A marine faithfully committed to counter-insurgency work. Believing – against the grain of public opinion – that serving as a marine's an imperative, a calling. But a marine who realised that he must himself spend time living in the sort of community desimated by ethnic conflict and hopelessness that is so often the seed-bed for terrorism.

In 2001, another year etched on the hard-drive of our hearts for the events of 9/11, this conviction led Barcott, a fledgling marine studying at the University of North Carolina, to go to Kibera in Kenya, Africa's largest and poorest slum, to live among its citizens, listen to their frustrations, but also hear their hopes, their plans to make it better, and to give assistance where he could. Out of this listening came Carolina for Kibera – an organisation enabling Kenyans to prevent the descent into terrorism through their own efforts to clean up and develop their community.

It's this Christ-like work that we hear about now, as we recall how the risen Jesus re-enters the hopelessness and despair of his disciples, following his death, to give them peace and to strengthen their faith.

Reading: John 20: 24-31

Thomas (who was called the Twin), one of the twelve, was not with them when Jesus came. So the other disciples told him, 'We have seen the Lord.' But he said to them, 'Unless I see the mark of the nails in his hands, and put my finger in the mark of the nails and my hand in his side, I will not believe.'

A week later his disciples were again in the house, and Thomas was with them. Although the doors were shut, Jesus came and stood among them and said, 'Peace be with you.' Then he said to Thomas, 'Put your finger here and see my hands. Reach out your hand and put it in my side. Do not doubt but believe.' Thomas answered him, 'My Lord and my God!' Jesus said to him, 'Have you believed because you have seen me? Blessed are those who have not seen and yet have come to believe.'

Now Jesus did many other signs in the presence of his disciples, which are not written in this book. But these are written so that you may come to believe that Jesus is the Messiah, the Son of God, and that through believing you may have life in his name.

That we may have life through Christ. That's the essence of the Gospel hope held out to us even on a day like this when we recall so much death and destruction. It's a belief that's indestructible because it's founded – as Rye Barcott discovered – on the grassroots being of God: a God, whose goodness, in the words of Archbishop Desmond Tutu, is stronger than evil, and who helps us to know that love and light are always stronger than the dark destructiveness of hatred.

Choir: Goodness is stronger than evil, Richard Tanner

Richard Tanner's setting of Desmond Tutu's words, leading us into our prayers.

So as we cling to the truth that goodness is stronger than evil we pray for all who mourn the loss of loved ones killed in the London terrorist attacks, as we recall those who continue to bear the scars in body, mind or spirit.

For all whose anger at injustice tempts them to seek revenge or to turn to violence and terror we seek the transforming love which is stronger than hate and the light that is stronger than darkness.

O Lord our heavenly Father, almighty and everlasting God, who hast safely brought us to the beginning of this day; defend us in the same with thy mighty power; and grant that this day we fall into no sin, neither run into any kind of danger, but that all our doings may be ordered by thy governance, to do always that is righteous in thy sight, through Jesus Christ our Lord. *Amen.*

We remember our calling to cherish the sanctity of life, the risen power of Christ over the forces of evil and death in a fallen world, the victory we are to proclaim through self-giving love, as we say the words that Jesus taught us: *Our Father ...*

Whatever we face, in confidence we turn to the Lord of all hopefulness, whose trust ever childlike no cares could destroy.

Hymn: Lord of all hopefulness

Remember, O Lord, what that hast wrought in us and not what we deserve: and as thou hast called us to thy service, so make us worthy of our calling; and the blessing of God Almighty, the Father, the Son and the Holy Spirit be amongst us, and remain with us always. *Amen.*

41. Learning for life: in company with God

5 September 2011

Choir: Alleluia, kindle in us the fire of your love, Margaret Rizza

Good morning.

When I was ordained a priest, the person leading the retreat – I forget now who it was which of course means they did a good job – gave each of us to be ordained a card. I've since mislaid it but not forgotten the sentiment expressed. God loves you like he loves no-one else. You love God like no-one else loves him. It said something important about the mutually-enriching, learning relationship each of us is called to have with God. But it rightly spoke of God's love first, which is what our hymn does now: Glorious things of thee are spoken.

Hymn: Glorious things

Let me glory in your name, O Lord. Let me know the lasting treasure of your love as I journey with you into the truth of your grace. *Amen.*

God loves me like he loves no-one else. I love God like no-one else loves him.

But the relationship is surely not so equal in reality? I mean for any of us to be who we are we actually need divine love, the affirmation of a hand laid on us, confirming that, sinful as we are, we are indeed accepted, cherished, nourished and sustained. But to be God he surely doesn't need my feeble attempts at loving, at reciprocating, at praying?

I think that's where a lot of people in my experience get to in their thinking and then give up! They hit a pretty obvious spiritual barrier – the truth that though there's mutuality about the relationship of God and any person, there's a difference of role, of function, of calling. To put it bluntly I'll always be a learner and God my teacher.

Something I learnt from Michael Mayne, that giant of Anglican spirituality, helps here. Since my part in the learning process, my job in the prayer by which this happens is to be silent. We place far too much store on intercessory prayer, the easiest, the most wordy, the most over-used sort of prayer. We literally batter the gates of heaven with what God knows already when real prayer and true relationship gets us past that me-ness, that demanding of God, and allows him to speak in the stillness, as it also allows us to answer God's call to be worshippers, to be those who acknowledge his worth, his place in our lives.

Reading: Psalm 19: 7-14

The law of the Lord is perfect, reviving the soul;
the decrees of the Lord are sure, making wise the simple;
the precepts of the Lord are right, rejoicing the heart;
the commandment of the Lord is clear, enlightening the eyes;
the fear of the Lord is pure, enduring for ever;
the ordinances of the Lord are true and righteous altogether.
More to be desired are they than gold, even much fine gold;
sweeter also than honey, and drippings of the honeycomb.
Moreover by them is your servant warned;
in keeping them there is great reward.
But who can detect their errors? Clear me from hidden faults.
Keep back your servant also from the insolent;
do not let them have dominion over me.
Then I shall be blameless, and innocent of great transgression.
Let the words of my mouth and the meditation of my heart be accept-
able to you, O Lord, my rock and my redeemer.

The psalms always hit the nail on the head. And the psalm

we've just heard takes us to the heart of our learning relationship with God. How do we know his perfection, his decrees, precepts, commandments and ordinances? How do we recognise them amidst the sinfulness of our lives? We do so when the words of our mouths give way to the meditation of our hearts and we discover our rock and redeemer speaking through us: a lamp for our feet and a light for our path.

Choir: Your word is a lamp, Margaret Rizza

Your word is a lamp to my feet and a light for my path, taking us into our prayers.

We pray for that word within us which gives us life, which dances in the stillness of our hearts.

We seek the grace we need to be silent and to wait for this word.

We pray that beyond the many concerns of a broken world – the cries of Libyans waking into freedom, or Somalians waking to hunger – we may hear the spirit interceding in us with sighs too deep for words.

We seek to hear the promptings of God in our lives as we say the prayer Jesus taught us to use: *Our Father ...*

So we look to travel with God in the daily journey of faith: One more step along the world I go.

Hymn: One more step

Keep us travelling with you, O Lord. Bless us with the strength of your courage and the power of your love, this day and evermore. *Amen.*

42. The extended 'family': All Saints

1 November 2011

Hymn: For all the saints (verse 1)

Good morning.

I almost felt I should've changed that greeting to Alleluia, echoing the choir on this All Saints Day. For how awesome are the saints, the heroes and heroines of the faith. How inspiring their witness. How varied and even eccentric the stories around them: Catherine on her wheel, Dunstan with his red tongs clipping Satan's powers, Swithun with his forty days of showers. And yet today isn't really so much about the named saints who have special days, it's for the unnamed ones, whose faith is known to God alone. Dare I think and say it, it's really a day for you and for me to consider being soldiers for Christ, faithful, true and bold.

Hymn: For all the saints (verses 3,4 and 7)

King of glory, help us to rise triumphant as the saints of this generation. Show us the more glorious day which comes when your kingdom breaks into the chaos of this world, through the gift of faith you nurture in us. *Amen.*

When Christians make a profession of faith they invariably express belief in a communion of saints. And I'm delighted that the council of Nicea plumped for the word communion when praising the saints and not for a word like family.

It's no bad thing to think about family of course – or to invoke – in moderation I would suggest, as not every one's experience of family is exactly positive – the language of family values – the theme for this week – or the concept of extended family which dovetails into today's celebration of All Saints.

But there's difficulty with the language of family that is over-come by the language of communion. And in my experience those churches which talk up family can institutionalise the dysfunc-tional behaviour that's a part of family life – head themselves into a cul-de-sac of perpetual adolescence – when what they are really seeking and needing to embrace is the mutuality, the responsibil-ity to and for one another, the deep connectedness which is wrapped up in that word communion. Because in a communion – and it's no coincidence we use the word to describe the moment we meet Jesus in bread and wine – everyone is of equal value and importance.

So communion of saints is actually the very best description – the best mission statement – we could have for the church since it suggests a mutually supportive group of people on a journey to-gether as learners in the school of holiness, the school that turns sinners, which is all of us, into saints. This is what all of us who claim the label Christian are, not just in embryo but in reality. Which places, as our reading from John's first epistle suggests, some considerable responsibility on us to recognise that wherever there's love, it's a sign of that communion binding together the children of God for the good of God's world.

Reading: 1 John 2: 29 – 3: 3

If you know that he is righteous, you may be sure that everyone who does right has been born of him. See what love the Father has given us, that we should be called children of God; and that is what we are. The reason the world does not know us is that it did not know him. Be-loved, we are God's children now; what we will be has not yet been revealed. What we do know is this: when he is revealed, we will be like him, for we will see him as he is. And all who have this hope in him purify themselves, just as he is pure.

Being pure as he is pure. That's the gift that true love cultivates in us. We see it when, in the image of the late seventeenth and early eighteenth century poet Isaac Watts, we screw up our eyes, allow ourselves to be tranported on the wings of faith God gives each of us, and see the saints above, in the joy and glory of the worship that unites them and us in a great communion of faith.

Choir: Give us the wings, Ernest Bullock

Ernest Bullock's setting of words by Isaac Watts, Give us the wings of faith, taking us into our prayers.

We pray for grace to know the victory of love in Jesus Christ, the victory which enables our fellowship with one another and with God to grow and to deepen.

So we pray for our communion with the saints in heaven, remembering the fractured and at times fractious nature of the saints in communion on earth.

As we express penitence for our divisions, we pray for a renewed sense of our unity in Christ, for the fruits of this in the love, joy and peace for which the world cries.

We remember all places of conflict. All communities facing persecution. We pray in our own society for a greater ability to meet deep divisions with conversation and a dialogue that honours and enhances our common humanity.

We pray for all who protest at injustice, for the prophetic ministry of the Church and for all whose task it is to ensure the safety and security of our citizens.

We express the hope that we may be God's saints as we work and pray for the coming of his kingdom in the words that Jesus taught us: *Our Father...*

We pray that we may be joined to the worship of the saints around the throne of grace as we raise the glad strain of praise. Ye watchers, and ye holy ones.

Hymn: Ye watchers and ye holy ones

As the saints rise triumphant to sing the song of God's praise, may this same God, Father, Son, and Holy Spirit, bless us his saints, this day and evermore. *Amen.*

43. Joy to the world: a fearless witness

26 December 2011

Good morning.

The Christmas box, a monetary gift for those in less-well-paid jobs – traditionally given today on Boxing Day – has taken a knock recently. The news that employment legislation might deem this gift a bribe has perhaps frightened some from giving it or made others more determined to do so. But either way the origin of giving the box lies in the fact that today is the feast of St Stephen, a deacon in the church, diakonos being the Greek word for servant. So today is the day to celebrate service, as the narrative of our opening carol reminds us with its invitation to look after those whom we should serve. Good King Wenceslas looked out on the feast of Stephen.

Hymn: Good King Wenceslas, arranged Reginald Jacques

Help us, O Lord, to receive your blessing by giving it as freely as you do, in our care for those who serve us so generously, and in our compassion for the needy, the suffering, and the persecuted. *Amen.*

For all its glitter the Christmas season has a starkness that challenges and confronts. A birth in a grotty stable after a bumpy journey on the back of a donkey is hardly what most mothers would wish. And as soon as angels and shepherds have arrived to see what has come to pass the Church takes us far outside the city of Jerusalem to watch as one of the earliest witnesses to the story of this baby is stoned to death for his faith. It's not where we expect to be. But as Jesus reminds his disciples in today's reading from Matthew's Gospel, though the cost of discipleship is fear and possible persecution, nothing can separate the faithful witness from the God who creates and loves them.

Reading: Matthew 10: 26-33

Jesus said to his disciples: 'So have no fear of them; for nothing is covered up that will not be uncovered, and nothing secret that will not become known. What I say to you in the dark, tell in the light; and what you hear whispered, proclaim from the housetops. Do not fear those who kill the body but cannot kill the soul; rather fear him who can destroy both soul and body in hell. Are not two sparrows sold for a penny? Yet not one of them will fall to the ground unperceived by your Father. And even the hairs of your head are all counted. So do not be afraid; you are of more value than many sparrows. 'Everyone therefore who acknowledges me before others, I also will acknowledge before my Father in heaven; but whoever denies me before others, I also will deny before my Father in heaven.

For his acknowledgement of the truth of Jesus Christ, Stephen is put on trial, accused of blasphemy – a charge still levelled at Christians today in some countries and one for which they pay a heavy price. Ironically, of course, his trial is at the behest of Saul of Tarsis, at this stage a busy persecutor of the followers of Jesus because he hasn't yet seen the light and been converted to Christ. The Paul whose letters we read is as yet some way off.

It's a complex story, one that the nineteen year old Rembrandt captures in his first painting, called The stoning of Stephen. It's in the Musée des arts in Lyon, and I remember looking at its cramped canvas, the walls of Jerusalem pressing in on the crowd gathered to stone this young man. He's dressed in a red dalmatic, the blood-red robe of a deacon, a servant, looking serenely upwards to the light shining on him from the heavens whilst around him hideously distorted faces lift stones to vent their anger. They do so of course simply because of the words he's uttered.

Words are powerful things. They can hurt very deeply and sometimes the hurt doesn't go away. Only the other day some words I'd said long ago in anger came back to haunt me as I met the person to whom I'd uttered them and realised that whatever they'd done for him they had actually damaged me. Which is why as we tell the story of our faith we must remember that the word is made flesh, not actually to be made word again – as is too often the case – but to live in hearts and imaginations. We show this word in our own flesh by who we are and how we serve not simply in what we say. "Preach the Gospel at all times," St Francis of Assisi said, "use words only when they're absolutely necessary." How I wish the church would remember that! How I wish I would too!

But when we have to use words let's make them loving and joyful ones, even if they put us at risk of rejection or suffering in a world that still often rejects real love. Go, tell it on the mountain that Jesus Christ is Lord.

Choir: Go tell it on the mountain, arranged Ken Burton

Go tell it on the mountain, arranged by Ken Burton, and taking us into our prayers.

We remember all who face persecution for their faith this day in countries across the world. For all unable either to practice or preach their faith freely. For all who are harried or harassed because of the integrity of their beliefs. For those living in constant anxiety and fear.

We pray for persecutors that the reality of the Gospel may cast out the fear in their hearts and bring them to know the power of love. May they, like Saul, be converted, transformed by the truth.

We pray for ourselves that we may have the courage to show love not only for the needy and the outcast but to every human soul, recognising that each is infinitely precious to God.

We pray especially at this time for all who feel persecuted by loneliness or by families filled with tension, bitterness or conflict.

May they know the comfort of the God who says do not be afraid.

As we reflect on the cost of the cradle, we pray for the coming of the Kingdom the Christ-child brings in the words that he taught us: *Our Father ...*

So as we give glory to God we turn again to the truth of Bethlehem and to the place where cradled in a manger, meanly laid the Son of Man his head

Hymn: Cradled in a manger

Send, O Lord, the joyful tidings of your Son's birth into every heart and home, that we may know the blessing of his love this day and evermore. *Amen.*

44. Shrove Tuesday: the common good

21 February 2012

Good morning.

In Alnwick in Northumberland, they'll be playing mob football. In St Columb Major in Cornwall the silver ball will be hurled. In Scarborough there'll be pancake racing with skipping ropes.

Today is Shrove Tuesday of course or mardi gras in many cultures – literally 'Fat Tuesday', a day when community life – the common good – is emphasised through indulgence in food and festivity, a day of excess before the rigours of the Lenten fast take over. It's a day that proclaims the kingdom to be near, and looks for its reality in a spirit of generosity that promises to change everything. Thy kingdom come! On bended knee the passing ages pray.

Hymn: Thy kingdom come! on bended knee

Help us, O God, to experience the perfect day of righteousness, your promised day, in this feast of fun and celebration. *Amen.*

Christians often give the impression of dourness. They aren't to be honest always the best of party animals. They major on sin and guilt, and a good deal else that might depress one's mood, and haven't taken very seriously the reality of a saviour who spent a good deal of his time at the dinner table as he partied his way round Galilee.

Of course there's a place for the dour and the serious. A cross on the forehead tomorrow, on Ash Wednesday, brings us down to earth with a crash that acknowledges the frailty of our humanity and the truth that each of us is a sinner in need of grace.

But it's the grace that Christians don't seem to make very attractive. Redemption is so often portrayed as if the headmaster is grudgingly giving a half-day holiday we're all jolly lucky to be receiving.

Of course we are jolly lucky to be getting it. But that's not the spirit in which it's given. God's love is boundless not qualified. It's eternal not given on a whim or a fancy, and least of all because any of us deserves it.

In my twenties, I spent five years looking after the choristers at King's College, Cambridge. And I remember joining on the same day as an eight year old boy who's now a cathedral assistant organist. I can still see him walking into King's College Chapel, looking up at that glorious fan-vaulted roof, and simply opening wide his eyes and mouth as he exclaimed with glee: "Wow!"

It was exactly the response that the architect must have envisaged. And which Wordsworth captured in a wonderful sonnet when looking at the roof he realised that it taught the mystery of generosity. "Give all thou canst" he writes, "high heaven rejects the lore of nicely calculated less or more". In other words – and to be dully prosaic – see the generosity of this roof, see it as built to God's glory, and respond by matching the spirit of its generosity. Let go and give everything to God too. Don't be stingy and say, "oo, you can have this but not that ... Give all thou canst". That's of course the spirit of party. The spirit that seeks the common good by trying to respond to God's unending generosity.

It's the spirit St Paul captures in our reading from 2 Corinthians chapter 9:

Reading: 2 Corinthians 9: 6-8, 11-14

The point is this: the one who sows sparingly will also reap sparingly, and the one who sows bountifully will also reap bountifully. Each of you must give as you have made up your mind, not reluctantly or under compulsion, for God loves a cheerful giver. And God is able to provide you with every blessing in abundance, so that by always having enough of everything, you may share abundantly in every good work. You will be enriched in every way for your great generosity, which will produce thanksgiving to God through us; for the rendering of this ministry not only supplies the needs of the saints but also over-flows with many thanksgivings to God. Through the testing of this ministry you glorify God by your obedience to the confession of the gospel of Christ and by the generosity of your sharing with them and with all others, while they long for you and pray for you because of the surpassing grace of God that he has given you.

God loves a cheerful giver. He wants us to be expansive in our generosity as he is always expansive. That means extending the party atmosphere to those for whom life is far from party-like. Give almes of thy goods and turn never thy face from any poor man.

Choir: Give almes of thy goods, Christopher Tye

Christopher Tye's setting of words from the book of Tobit, Give almes of thy goods, words used as the offering is brought to the altar in a communion service, and taking us into our prayers:

We pray that our generosity of spirit may promote the common good, may bind the poor and the marginalised, the lonely and the distressed, to the heart of the community, in one unbroken fellow-ship of love.

We pray for nations where a sense of community and common good is fractured by a spirit of selfishness and oppression, of mis-ery and conflict. We remember especially at this time the people of Syria.

We pray that the fun of Shrove Tuesday may carry us into the Lenten fast with spirits renewed in God's grace.

A prayer of John V Taylor:

Spirit of God, Lord and giver of life, moving between us and around, like wind or water or fire; breathe into us your freshness that we may awake; cleanse our vision that we may see more clearly; kindle our senses that we may feel more sharply; and give us the courage to live as you would have us live, through Jesus Christ our Lord. *Amen.*

We pray that we may experience the fullness of the kingdom praying the words that Jesus taught us: *Our Father ...*

We lift our hearts to God as we express thanks for all the gifts we receive through his bounty: Praise to the Lord, the almighty, the king of creation

Hymn: Praise to the Lord, the Almighty the king of creation

Let the amen of praise and adoration sound from your people, O Lord, as you bless us with your grace, this day and evermore. *Amen.*

45. Act of Worship: Easter and Sarajevo

13 April 2012

Good morning.

The week after Easter Day is meant traditionally to be a quiet one for clergy like myself, a time to draw breath after the rigours of Holy Week. But the realisation that it's twenty years since the start of the siege of Sarajevo – and the many reflective articles that have drawn attention to this – has actually made it a disquietening time for me. Easter's promise of new life and hope – and the vacuous smiliness which often accompanies assertions of this – has immediately been confronted with the harsh reality of humans at their worst, on our continent of Europe, just two decades ago. It means that the Alleluias somewhat lose their sheen and I'm left like so many wondering whether the brighter dawn to which our opening hymn bears witness is indeed breaking?

Hymn: A brighter dawn is breaking

O free the world from blindness, Lord, and fill the world with kindness. As you promise to give sinners resurrection, and to bring our striving to perfection, help us to face the truth of a world in constant conflict and to embrace the change that's needed to transform it into your kingdom of peace and justice. Amen.

Within a few weeks of the beginning of the siege of Sarajevo, and as bombs rained down on that beautiful university city, churches, synagogues, mosques, historic buildings, concert halls and homes had been damaged or destroyed. There was soon very little food left for the city's population. But people nonetheless queued morning and afternoon in the city's squares waiting for the truck to come and for whatever bread may be on it.

185

One morning, as the clock struck ten and without warning, a mortar shell exploded inches away from one such queue. As the injured cried out for help and those who lived in close-by houses rushed out to assist them, snipers fired volleys of shots, prolonging the horror and injuring some of those who were there to help.

A few minutes later, as the survivors surveyed the scene, they began to count the bodies of twenty-two of their fellow Sarajevans who now lay dead on the ground.

Beyond immediate help for the injured, the collection of bodies, and comfort for the bereaved, one of the men who'd rushed out to assist wondered what could be done amid this senseless madness? His answer seemed to echo the instruction that Moses gave when a plague had arisen and he'd sent the priest Aaron with his incense burner to stand in the gap between the living and the dead, with amazing consequences.

Reading: Numbers 16: 46-48

Moses said to Aaron, 'Take your censer, put fire on it from the altar and lay incense on it, and carry it quickly to the congregation and make atonement for them. For wrath has gone out from the Lord; the plague has begun.' So Aaron took it as Moses had ordered, and ran into the middle of the assembly, where the plague had already begun among the people. He put on the incense, and made atonement for the people. He stood between the dead and the living; and the plague was stopped.

When life becomes cross-shaped, as so often it seems to, someone needs to take the initiative, seize courage with both hands and stand in the gap. Sometimes this is to stop people fighting. It means literally standing between people amidst the conflict as officials of the United Nations are doing today in Syria now that a ceasefire has been established and is, hopefully, being respected. This is how resurrection comes to complex situations. Vacuous, smiley assurances that all will be well don't usually produce the results that are desired and needed. Someone has to reassert – in however small a way – that conflict and violence is the not the final word on what it means to be human.

Which is where what happened as the clock struck ten the day after that mortar attack in Sarajevo is so instructive. For emerging from one of the doorways onto the square where 22 of his fellow Sarajevans had been massacred the day before came one of the men who'd rushed to help the survivors and who'd spent all night wondering what on earth he could do in response. Dressed in white tie and tails, he carried a small stool in one hand and a 'cello case in the other, as he moved to sit in the crater where the mortar shell fell and to begin to play. He was too upset at first to know quite what he was playing but suddenly he realised that his bow and fingers were shaping into sound the famous melody of Albinoni's Adagio, a melody actually found in the ruins of Dresden during the Second World War when allied bombing destroyed one of that city's many libraries.

Like Aaron before him, this thirty-seven-year-old man, Vedran Smailovic, a cellist in the Sarajevo Opera Orchestra, was actually standing in the gap between death and resurrection because it's only literally by making such a stand for peace that its shoots begin to emerge.

Music: from Adagio in G minor, Tomoso Albinoni

John V Taylor, a former bishop of Winchester, once asserted: 'a ripple of light... the lift of a heart suddenly less lonely is all the Easter evidence I ask.' As the melody from Albinoni's famous Adagio echoes within us, we move into prayer, giving thanks for the ripples of light from those like Vedran Smailovic who step into the cross-shaped gaps in our world, the places of conflict and misery, and begin to transform them simply by being there.

We pray for the people of Bosnia, remembering the uneasy relationships that exist between Bosniak, Croat and Serb, Muslim, Catholic and Orthodox.

We remember the unresolved issues from this and many conflicts, the wrongs unacknowledged, the bodies undiscovered, the hurts unhealed.

We pray for a more sensitive and less bombastic witness to the hope of resurrection, one that works through pain to discover the possibility for light and hope.

We pray for those in trauma at this time, as a result of natural disaster in Indonesia, war in Syria, civil strife in Nigeria.

We look to the hope that is in Christ as we say the prayer that he taught us: Our Father ...

We look with thankfulness for the signs of resurrection in the world: Now the green blade rises from the buried grain

Hymn: Now the green blade rises

May God's touch call us all back to the fullness of his life as he embraces us with his compassion and love, and may the blessing of God Almighty, the Father, the Son, and the Holy Spirit, be with us this Eastertide and evermore. Amen.

46. Act of Worship: Christian Aid Week

11 May 2012

Good morning.

There's inevitably been lots of focus this past week on the beginning of a new parliamentary session and the speech by Her Majesty The Queen that traditionally starts it. What the speech might contain, what it did contain, and for those not in the Coalition – maybe some in the parties involved too – what they think it should have contained.

Seven minutes of speech listing fifteen bills and four draft bills, inevitably produces hours of debate. And it's healthy – if rather repetitive and perhaps overly partisan at times – to rehearse the arguments for and against as our parliamentarians discuss the direction of travel our society is or should be taking, and discern how this might best be reflected in public policy.

Beyond possible reform of the House of Lords or the complex issues around our double-dip recession in Britain or the perilous financial state of our neighbours in continental Europe, I found it encouraging that the issue of how much money we commit as a nation to international aid and development also came to the fore.

A promise that 0.7 per cent of our GDP, our gross domestic product, would be set aside for this, was made a couple of years ago and many think that it should be enshrined in law. Whatever the merits of such a move, however, the fact that we're reviewing what is set aside – it's inevitably a hotly contested issue in such cash-strapped times – is surely good just at the point when that hardy annual for the British Churches, and many others, Christian Aid Week, is upon us in just two days time. For with this week each year – its door to door collections, and the many events and services it inspires – comes a focus on the developing world and especially on how those of us more financially fortunate may partner a financially disadvantaged but resource-rich continent like Africa, for instance, to help our neighbours there develop their fullest potential.

Music: Goodness is stronger than evil, James Whitbourn

Lord Jesus, help us to make the hope of those words of Desmond Tutu a reality in your world. May all your children know the victory which you win for us through your cross and resurrection over poverty and disease, greed and selfishness. May each experience light and life, as together we enjoy the goodness and fullness of your love. Amen.

I've just returned from a visit to Cape Town – I think it's the forty-sixth time I've been there! So Africa is inevitably on my mind as it long ago worked itself into my heart, hence that beautiful setting in a thoroughly South African style of Desmond Tutu's words. But it wasn't so much the issues of South Africa, as its neighbour Zimbabwe that struck me on this trip.

I don't drive, so I'm reliant on the craziness of mini-bus taxis to get me around the Cape Peninsula or, if these aren't available, the much more expensive – and less dangerous – metered taxis.

Almost all of these seem now to be being driven by Zimbabweans rather than Capetonians.

I chatted to a man from Marandera, for example, an enchantingly beautiful region in Zimbabwe, who had a doctorate in civil engineering but who had fled Zimbabwe four years ago when he could take the chaos of President Robert Mugabe's rule no longer.

He was one of three doctors now unable to use their amazing giftedness and driving taxis in Cape Town instead – taxis which charge a fortune to their passengers but whose drivers see next to nothing of the takings. The civil engineer I've mentioned was complimented by a theologian from Harare who'd researched the impact of churches on community development and a lawyer from Bulawayo specialising in human rights.

I was also driven by two people with Masters degrees, by several lawyers, a medical doctor, countless Harare business people, entrepeneurs and a handful of teachers, once part of Africa's best schooling system – actually created by Mugabe, the former teacher with a genuine passion for education, which he then destroyed.

Each had a story to tell. One had swum a crocodile-infested lake to cross into South Africa. Some had bribed border guards. All had family back home after whom they waited anxiously for news. Many recounted how they'd fled beatings and deprivation then to find rejection, abuse and hardship at the hands of some South Africans who felt that here was a group stealing their livelihoods.

Rarely were these narratives easy listening. But they all had one striking feature in common. Whatever the suffering endured, each of these taxi drivers still passionately believed in the possibility that things could and would be better. Each had gifts they knew one day they would use again.

Like the Jesus of the Fourth Gospel they sought – indeed in many ways they already knew – that fullness of life about which John chapter 10 speaks so eloquently.

Reading: John 10: 7-11

Jesus said to the disciples, 'Very truly, I tell you, I am the gate for the sheep. All who came before me are thieves and bandits; but the sheep did not listen to them. I am the gate. Whoever enters by me will be saved, and will come in and go out and find pasture. The thief comes only to steal and kill and destroy. I came that they may have life, and have it abundantly. 'I am the good shepherd. The good shepherd lays down his life for the sheep.

Life in abundance, life in all its fullness, however the dynamism of the Greek is translated, it's what those determined to see a percentage of our GDP spent on international aid and development are seeking, it's what development and aid agencies are advocating, it's what one in the field sets as it's Gospel objective: every person, every community, a full life. It's surely what each of us wants for ourselves and for our neighbours wherever they are.

But life in its fullness is modelled by the one who also lays down his life for the sheep. It comes at a cost. It involves sacrifice. That is after all what the generosity invoked and invited in Christian Aid week is all about.

Music: A South African Prayer, James Whitbourn

Lord help me to give myself when I am giving, words of the South African novelist and anti-apartheid activist, Alan Paton, set to music by James Whitbourn, and taking us into our prayers.

Help us Lord to give of ourselves when we are giving, to give without thought of receiving and to receive without thought of giving.

Help us to work in true partnership with our neighbours, and to see a continent like Africa not simply as an index of human poverty and misery but for the place of enterprise and entrepreneurship, ideas and imagination you have already made it.

Bless the work of all development, aid and mission agencies that they may hoard nothing of the riches you unlock through them save the love they are to share for the good of all.

Unlock in each of us a deeper understanding of our responsibility to and for our neighbours, and an openness to learn and receive from them.

Make us true partners in your Gospel of generosity and love as we share the prayer your Son taught us: *Our Father ...*

Brother, sister, let me serve you, let me be as Christ to you.

Music: The Servant Song, Richard Gillard

Bless us, O Lord, with the grace to serve and to be served, that in Christ we may be Christ to one another, this day and evermore. Amen.

47. The God who asks: different kinds of service

13 June 2012

Good morning.

When he writes to the church in Philippi, St Paul says that God loves a cheerful giver. He could just as easily have exhorted them to be cheerful doers or carers. However it's put, there's a practical edge which is fundamental to Christian witness. At times it can all seem to get lost in the realm of the cerebral – at turns naval-gazing or high fallutin' or just plain incomprehensible – but as important as the thinking stuff is in religion, discipleship is meant to work itself out in service, inspired of course by the one who came not to be served but to serve: Son of God, eternal Saviour.

Hymn: Son of God, eternal Saviour

Son of God and Son of Man, as your presence in heaven inspires our worship and devotion, and your presence on earth hallows our human nature, link us all in prayer and service for the common good. *Amen.*

Just at the moment we're hearing quite a lot about people who make a practical difference in the community. Our focus as a nation on The Queen's Diamond Jubilee has inevitably brought words like dedication and service to the fore as we've reflected on what it means to give oneself for the care of neighbour and stranger alike.

When The Queen's birthday honours' list is published this coming weekend we'll celebrate all sorts of people who've done so in our local communities. There'll be those who've given up hours of time for charity or to run a scout troop or a brownie pack. All of these stories must be cherished and celebrated as we trumpet the voluntary principle they illustrate, which makes such a difference to our communities. But I wonder if there's not a danger in some of the language that's being used. Because increasingly voluntary service is being contrasted with financial service – what's given freely is being set against what's earned in monetary terms – as if these were mutually exclusive spheres of activity.

There's inevitably – and rightly – anger at the greed of some in our society whose bonuses seem wildly unrealistic – indeed obscene to many – in the face of austerity Britain, and the fact that a majority are really feeling the pinch. And the Bible certainly has plenty to say on the subject. But what it says about money concerns its proper use. It doesn't attack the making of money per se as if somehow to be a banker, for instance, is in itself to inhabit some shady under-world where the devil reigns.

Added to which – and from our own recent experience as a nation – we know that the business of caring for others – especially the most vulnerable and needy – can be seen as just that, a business that forgets it's about people. It can be just as susceptible then of abuse as money-lenders and -makers. So I wonder if what we need to do, instead of slamming bad bankers and bad carers – is to re-explore the right relationship, indeed the inter-relationship, between money and care. Of course this is hardly new territory.

Whenever you start to run something – as the earliest disciples discovered when the entity we call the church began to emerge – you soon discover that your caring mission needs cash.

Reading: 1 Corinthians 16: 1-4

Now concerning the collection for the saints: you should follow the directions I gave to the churches of Galatia. On the first day of every week, each of you is to put aside and save whatever extra you earn, so that collections need not be taken when I come. And when I arrive, I will send any whom you approve with letters to take your gift to Jerusalem. If it seems advisable that I should go also, they will accompany me.

A principle of giving is being bashed out here – first in Galatia and then in Corinth – which can't be turned into an easy formula. Though there was plenty of precedent in the Hebrew scriptures, in relation to tithing, for instance, we don't quite know how those earliest Christians set about deciding what was extra to their normal earnings. There must have been then – as there is now – pretty heated discussion about the financial nitty-gritty. But we do know that the concept of a common good trumped every other concern. Cash and care were set in the context of a wider objective – the happiness and wholeness, the love and loving-kindness of the community. Ubi caritas et amor, Deus ibi est. Where there is love and loving-kindness, God is there.

Choir: Ubi caritas et amor, Maurice Duruflé

Maurice Duruflé's setting of the antiphon Ubi caritas, et amor, Deus ibi est, where there is love and living-kindness, God is there, and taking us into our prayers.

We pray for wisdom in the use of the gifts and resources that God entrusts to each person and community.

We ask that inequality may be met with generosity.

We remember all who struggle financially at this time, all who are isolated and seemingly without carers, and all whose burden is heavy because of the duty of care that they exercise.

We pray for those who work in financial or in caring professions that each may act with integrity for the common good.

We pray especially for all injured by the bombing today in Iraq, those caring for them as also for the bereaved.

We recognise the opportunities for love and service which God entrusts to us as we say the words that Jesus taught us:
Our Father ...

As we look to the coming of the kingdom in its fullness we proclaim God's embrace for the whole world: Go forth and tell! O Church of God, awake!

Hymn: Go forth and tell! O Church of God, awake!

Bless us, as we go in your strength, Lord, to serve you, this day and evermore. *Amen.*

48. Act of Worship: the power of a handshake

29 June 2012

Good morning.

Shaking hands has a long history maybe to the beginnings of human life itself. Certainly we have surviving depictions of a handshake between two Greek soldiers and another between two Greek gods as early as the fifth century before Christ. We don't know their meaning but we may hazzard a guess that in both instances the shake of a hand indicates peace. The cultural historians and anthropologists suggest that a handshake between former enemies was a clear sign that they had no weapons.

When Her Majesty The Queen and the Deputy First Minster of Northern Ireland, Martin McGuiness, shook hands earlier this week, as part of The Queen's Diamond Jubilee tour, weapons were not of course an issue. But they had been, since Mr McGuiness was once a senior commander in the Irish Republican Army, the IRA, which had taken up weapons in their campaign to end British rule in the Province. This campaign of course touched the Royal Family personally when Earl Mountbatten of Burma was assassinated in 1979. But as The Queen acknowledged last year on her historic state visit to the Irish Republic – when she offered her "sincere thoughts and deep sympathies" to the victims on all sides, it had produced pain for Britain and for Ireland.

So the handshake bore a depth of meaning far beyond its brevity. It was unthinkable amidst the troubles in the 70s and 80s and even perhaps five years ago, a long way into the Good Friday Agreement, that was bringing republicans and nationalists together for the common good. But it happened and it was a sign of reconciliation, peace and hope.

Hymn: Lord of all hopefulness

Give us your peace Lord, as we use our hands to worship you in prayer, to do your work, to express care and friendship, to reach out in reconciliation and love. Amen.

Handshakes have, as I've suggested, a deep symbolic power. They are at once a moment of greeting and meeting – as on this occasion Martin McGuiness offered The Queen the 'hundred thousand welcomes' traditional in Ireland – a moment that brings people into contact and, in this case, express a new unity of purpose. But they're also pregnant with future possibility. They suggest both a point of convergence and a journey yet to be walked. Richard Nixon and Mao Tse Tung, Anwar Sadat and Menchem Begin, Ronald Reagan and Mikhail Gorbachev, David Trimble and John Hume, Nelson Mandela and FW de Klerk.

We remember the handshakes they exchanged because they inaugurated something new, something hoped for, longed for even, and also something to be worked at. Sometimes of course the journey that follows the scene on the White House lawn or wherever is not an easy one. It falters and sadly – as is the case in the Middle East right now – sometimes fails to deliver on its promises. But the instinct to reach out and to reconcile, to transcend enmity and bitterness in the search for peace is as old and deep as the world itself.

It surely comes from the God who's engraved each and every one of us on the palms of his hands as we're reminded in our reading from Isaiah chapter 49.

Reading: Isaiah 49: 13-18:

Sing for joy, O heavens, and exult, O earth; break forth, O mountains, into singing! For the Lord has comforted his people, and will have compassion on his suffering ones. But Zion said, 'The Lord has forsaken me, my Lord has forgotten me.' Can a woman forget her nursing-child, or show no compassion for the child of her womb? Even these may forget, yet I will not forget you. See, I have inscribed you on the palms of my hands; your walls are continually before me.

Your builders outdo your destroyers, and those who laid you waste go away from you. Lift up your eyes all around and see; they all gather, they come to you. As I live, says the Lord, you shall put all of them on like an ornament, and like a bride you shall bind them on.

There's so much imagery in that passage that resonates with this week's handshake, from the joy it gave to the communities represented through the memories of suffering and abandonment that also came with it, not least for those most deeply affected by the troubles – including Her Majesty The Queen herself – and on to the hope that 'destroyers become builders' are putting peace into each others' hands and learning to walk a new journey as they gather together around a shared hope.

Hymn: Put peace into each others' hands

Put peace into each others' hands, a reflective hymn taking us into our prayers (spoken over the Taizé chant, My peace I leave you)

We give thanks to God for the courage and leadership of so many who have sought to rebuild what was destroyed in Northern Ireland.

We remember the pain and cost of the journey walked. The lives lost, the injuries inflicted, the grief and suffering still borne by many.

We celebrate the courage of all who takes risks for peace in Northern Ireland and throughout the world.

We look to the coming of the kingdom of peace in all its fulness as we say the words that Jesus taught us: Our Father ...

We embrace the search for truth and peace in our own lives, as we build new hope in our communities: I would be true for there are those who trust me.

Hymn: I would be true

Help us to look up to the vision you set before us, to laugh and love and live as you bless us with your peace this day and evermore. Amen.

49. Training for life: faithful devotion

23 July 2012

Good morning.

We're just days away from the opening of the thirtieth Olympiad, the Olympic Games 2012, and the excitement is certainly building in London. The torch arrived a few days ago and is wending its way through the streets of the city's boroughs. I'm here in London, so as I made my way to the studio this morning I felt a tingle down my spine as I saw the flags of the two hundred and four participating nations strung from building to building all down Oxford Street. This week on Daily Service we pick up the Olympic theme as we focus on training for life and today think of the faithful devotion that's needed to take this forward. The Bible is somewhat devoid of sporting metaphors but 'running the race of life' – one of the better ones – is tucked away in several of Paul's letters. It's the basis of our first hymn: Fight the good fight with all thy might.

Hymn: Fight the good fight

In running the race you set before us, O Lord, help us not to faint nor to fear but only to believe that you are with us, and in us. Amen.

If any city requires trust in God and the faithful devotion of its citizens, its Mogadishu in Somalia, one of the world's most lawless places, in a country devastated now by civil war for over twenty years. But from within it this last week two athletes emerged with a story that will surely be one of the most moving from the rich narrative of this year's Olympiad.

201

The journey to London 2012 was never going to be easy for the only athletes being sent by the Somalian Olympic Association, Zamzam Mohamed Farah, who competes in the women's Four hundred metres and Mohammed Hassan Mohammed Taylow who takes his place in the Men's Fifteen hundred metre line up.

They've had to train along the bullet-ridden streets of Mogadishu. They've braved explosions and attacks by extremist groups fighting Somalian Government forces and African Union troops. And they've described their venues for training as "simply unimaginable" compared to those enjoyed by many an Olympic athlete. Almost every sports facility in Somalia has been destroyed during the long years of conflict and the equipment available has been less than rudimentary. British tabloids have run story after story about the logistical problems of the games. They seem to wish failure on the enterprise instead of to celebrate this extraordinary festival of global humanity. But the presence of these Somalian heroes is surely a sign of amazingly faithful devotion to a task, of overcoming incredible hardship just to run the race. Yet it's more than this. It's testament to the honour and responsibility that comes with giving hospitality to such a diverse group of people. The Games takes us to the heart of the Christian faith where story-telling and hosting go hand in hand day by day, week by week in the Eucharist when we remember and experience today the power of Jesus as present now as he was at the Last Supper. But it also bears witness to the central event of our faith, to a belief that conflict and death are never the final word. They are always swallowed up in the hope and the reality of resurrection.

Let's remind ourselves what it means to be a witness to that truth now as we join Mary Magdalen – whose feast day fell yesterday – at the tomb on the first Easter morning, Mark's Gospel tells the story.

Reading: Mark 15: 47-16: 8

Mary Magdalen and Mary the mother of Joses saw where the body was laid. When the sabbath was over, Mary Magdalen, and Mary the mother of James, and Salome bought spices, so that they might go and anoint him. And very early on the first day of the week, when the sun had risen, they went to the tomb. They had been saying to one another, 'Who will roll away the stone for us from the entrance to the tomb?' When they looked up, they saw that the stone, which was very large, had already been rolled back. As they entered the tomb, they saw a young man, dressed in a white robe, sitting on the right side; and they were alarmed. But he said to them, 'Do not be alarmed; you are looking for Jesus of Nazareth, who was crucified. He has been raised; he is not here. Look, there is the place they laid him. But go, tell his disciples and Peter that he is going ahead of you to Galilee; there you will see him, just as he told you.' So they went out and fled from the tomb, for terror and amazement had seized them; and they said nothing to anyone, for they were afraid.

Like the first witnesses to resurrection there's probably much that Somalia's two Olympians cannot put into words about the complexity of their journey to hope. But what certainly shines through is their faithfulness, their trust in a power beyond themselves. I would be true for there are those who trust me.

Hymn: I would be true

Howard Arnold Walter's words, I would be true, to Percy Grainger's arrangement of the Londonderry Air, and taking us into our prayers

We give thanks for the faithful witness of so many to the possibility of resurrection in the world.

We pray for those places in the world and situations where signs of hope are so desperately longed-for. We hold before God all devastated by the loss of loved ones in the Arora shooting in Colorado.

We celebrate the spirit of hope represented in the Olympic ideal, the athletes and officials assembling from all over the globe.

We pray for all responsible for their safety and security and for the many spectators who will join them.

Almighty God you created humanity in your image and delight in our talent, skill and flair: give us grace to celebrate the achievements of our fellow men and women. Give determination and equity to competitors, gratitude and charm to winners, grace and mercy to those who do not come first, and thankfulness and admiration to observers, that in all our best efforts your creation may be glorified. Amen.

We offer our own longing for resurrection in whatever situations we find ourselves as we say the prayer that Jesus taught us: Our Father ...

As we celebrate Olympic talent, so we look to follow faithfully the giver of all gifts: O Jesus, I have promised to serve thee to the end.

Hymn: O Jesus, I have promised

Guide us, O Lord, call us and draw us along the road that leads to the fullness of the resurrection life with which you bless us now. Amen.

50. The commandments: the sabbath

4 September 2012

Good morning.

'The child who's born on the sabbath day is bonny and blithe and good and gay.' Like me you probably learned that rhyme as a child. Its language was dated then but it seems positively prehistoric now! Not least that word sabbath sticks out doesn't it. Who talks much about the sabbath these days? But amidst the commandments that are our focus this week in Daily Service it's today's theme. And its twin function as a day of rest and a day to praise God is hinted at in our first hymn: Awake my soul and with the sun thy daily stage of duty run.

Hymn: Awake my soul, and with the sun

Help us, O Lord, to make that prayer our own, to praise you from whom every blessing in life flows, to join our prayers and praises with the whole of creation, and to focus anew on the gift and possibility of your kingdom. Amen.

We're a long way from 1924 and the controversy caused by Eric Lidell, a Scottish athlete and later missionary to China, who refused to break the sabbath day by running in the Olympic Games that year in Paris. He swapped Olympic events with Harold Abrahams, a Jewish colleague, and both of course won gold as Chariots of Fire, the film now revived as a stage play in London, so poignantly recounts.

It was Sunday trading that finally did for the identity of Sunday – the Christian sabbath – in the United Kingdom. And people like me still regret the spinelessness that the leaders of the Church of England of which I'm a priest showed at the time.

Some may find that judgement harsh but if you review what was said in the early 90s, when the idea was being debated, many got excited, for example, about the impact on car-parking around their churches due to the increased number of shoppers, or on the numbers of people attending, due to absences by those involved in retail, but very few were really making the fundamental point that for the health and well-being of society – and to ensure that workers are not exploited – we need a day for recreation. A day to recreate our sense of perspective. A day to redirect our attention to those sustaining values and commitments which are learned through the spaciousness of worship as through the space we make simply to be quiet and to reflect.

Of course, when it had the space and an audience perhaps literally more captive, the church could make a hash of using it. Go back to the 1948 Olympic Games and you find that on the one Sunday that fell during the games – when the athletes were encouraged to go to church – had they attended St Paul's Cathedral here in London they would have heard the Archbishop of Canterbury at the time, Geoffrey Fisher, recommend that using donors for the artificial insemination of humans be made a criminal offence! Never let it be said that the church isn't capable of missing the chance to connect and to resonate! Though if you'd gone to St Paul's Cathedral a couple of Sundays ago you'd have seen wheelchair basketball beneath the dome during a service for the Paralympic Games.

But whether the church gets it right or not the truth remains that a day for a different kind of attentiveness both within ourselves and to the transcendent truths of life is essential, as chapter 20 of the Book of the Exodus reminds us:

Reading: Exodus 20: 8-11

Remember the sabbath day, and keep it holy. For six days you shall labour and do all your work. But the seventh day is a sabbath to the Lord your God; you shall not do any work—you, your son or your daughter, your male or female slave, your livestock, or the alien resident in your towns. For in six days the Lord made heaven and earth, the sea, and all that is in them, but rested the seventh day; therefore the Lord blessed the sabbath day and consecrated it.

I'm not one of those who thinks – with Eric Lidell – that the sabbath should only be for church. I think we need a much wider concept of recreation than this. Though I do think that six opportunities a week for retail therapy is quite enough for anyone. But as one who lives in a household where the tension between football and church is a real one for a second son who is a passionate member of a local team, I know only too well the importance of cultivating the key feature of recreation which is attentiveness. Whether its watching David Weir's arms as he powers himself to victory in the 5000 metres in the Paralymic Games, or the blades of Oscar Pistorius or the extraordinary power of Elie Simmonds' tiny limbs – all incidentally on a Sunday – what's being learned is the poet's ability, the worshipper's ability to sense something new. Eyes are being lifted and hearts are being raised to see something never perhaps before noticed about the nature of what it means to be human. And from this comes the point of sabbath – that we too may be made fully alive, fully human, risen with Christ to a new life in him.

Hymn: I lift my eyes

Bishop Timothy Dudley Smith's words, I lift my eyes to the quiet hills, set to music by Elizabeth Crocker and Bishop Michael Baughen: a meditation on the need to bring the principle of sabbath into our everyday lives, and taking us into our prayers.

We pray for an ability to pause amidst the busyness of life , to take stock, to reflect, to refocus and to recreate a vision of human living for ourselves and for our neighbours.

We seek anew the opportunity to celebrate all that is good in life remembering that the Christian sabbath is the day of resurrection. We give special thanks at this time for the rich truths that our Paralympians are teaching us, through the excellence of their pursuit of glory.

We remember all who are marginalised, who lack such opportunity, who crave someone to notice them, to encourage and support their journey to wholeness and holiness.

We ask that we be given grace to hold the still voice of God at the centre of our lives, and to redirect ourselves to his presence as we do his will. Especially at this time we pray for all affected by the rioting in Belfast and for those seeking to bring peace there, as we say the prayer that Jesus taught us: Our Father ...

We look to the new life that comes from our moments of sabbath rest and reflection: The Day of Resurrection! Earth, tell it out abroad.

Hymn: The Day of Resurrection

May we know the joy that has no end, may we sing the song of resurrection in our lives, may God bless us with the risen presence of Christ, this day and evermore. Amen.

51. A jazz celebration for Pentecost

4 June 2006

Continuity announcement:
And now Sunday Worship – a celebration for Pentecost from Blackburn Cathedral. The service, which will include Bob Chilcott's Little Jazz Mass, is led by the Dean of Blackburn, The Very Reverend Christopher Armstrong and the preacher is Canon Chris Chivers. It begins with the Introit, The Spirit is moving in my heart.

Choir: The Spirit is moving in my heart, Galloway

Welcome, The Dean:
As the Spirit moves in the hearts of people across the globe, so we welcome you to Blackburn Cathedral for this Jazz Eucharist on the Feast of Pentecost, in which we use offbeat rhythms, improvised melodies, the sheer exuberance of Jazz to give thanks for the gift to us of God's Holy Spirit.

Like the first apostles, we've gathered all together in one place to celebrate the fulfilment of God's promise that the Spirit of the Lord will be upon each of us so that the world may be renewed and transformed by love.

Reading, Acts 2: 1-4, Emma Pearson:
When the day of Pentecost had come, the apostles were all together in one place. And suddenly from heaven there came a sound like the rush of a violent wind, and it filled the entire house where they were sitting. Divided tongues, as of fire, appeared among them, and a tongue rested on each of them. All of them were filled with the Holy Spirit and began to speak in other languages, as the Spirit gave them ability.

The Dean:
So we pray for grace to learn the language of the Spirit as we sing the hymn, Come down, O Love Divine

Hymn: Come down, O Love divine.

Penitence, The Dean:
Mindful that we are far from perfect yet hopeful that the breath of God's Spirit will bring us to wholeness of life, let us confess our sins.

Lord, have mercy
Christ, have mercy
Lord, have mercy

Absolution, The Dean:
Come Holy Spirit, fill the hearts of your people, forgive us our sins, and kindle within us the fire of your love. *Amen.*

The Dean:
Glory to God in the highest and peace to His people on earth!

Choir: Gloria, Chilcott

Collect, The Dean:
Let us pray:

Holy Spirit, sent by the Father,
ignite in us your holy fire;
strengthen your children with the gift of faith,
revive your Church with the breath of love,
and renew the face of the earth,
through Jesus Christ our Lord. *Amen.*

Gospel: Luke 4:16-21, Jonathan Turner

When Jesus came to Nazareth, where he had been brought up, he went to the synagogue on the Sabbath day, as was his custom. He stood up to read, and the scroll of the prophet Isaiah was given to him. He un-rolled the scroll and found the place where it was written:
'The Spirit of the Lord is upon me,
because he has anointed me
to bring good news to the poor.
He has sent me to proclaim release to the captives
and recovery of sight to the blind,
to let the oppressed go free,
to proclaim the year of the Lord's favour.'
And he rolled up the scroll, gave it back to the attendant, and sat down. The eyes of all in the synagogue were fixed on him. Then he began to say to them, 'Today this scripture has been fulfilled in your hearing.'

Sermon, Canon Chris Chivers:
The composer Handel once said that what the English like is music 'they can beat time to … something that hits them straight on the drum of the ear'. The conductor Thomas Beecham was per-haps less complimentary. He suggested that the British 'may not like music, but they absolutely love the noise that it makes'. I'm not sure what Handel and Beecham would have made of contem-porary society in all its rich diversity – its religions and cultures each contributing something very distinctive and vital to our sense not just of local or national but of international, of global identity. How, I wonder, would they have viewed nations – and faith com-munities within them – which now embrace classical and jazz, hip-hop and soul? And what would they – what do we – make of the energy, the vibrancy, of the spirit behind all this? The spirit we call holy, whose presence is celebrated on this day of Pentecost?

I well remember as an ordinand being in a parish where one of the churchwardens warned the Vicar in hushed tones of the ad-vent of the Toronto blessing. She'd clearly seen dramatic television reports of North American preachers summoning forth spirit-filled

phenomena in convention halls filled with thousands of worshippers. 'People are being literally blown onto their backs by the
Spirit', she informed him. 'Well, we don't want the Holy Spirit in
here, do we?' he replied mischievously, adding, with an irony she
didn't seem quite to grasp: 'If I were you I should make sure that
all the doors and windows are shut.'

We seem to prefer to plan for the Holy Spirit's presence or to
invoke it only when it fits in with our plans, rather than to be overwhelmed by the unsettling dynamism of the great disturber. Yet
despite our attempts to control or to stop the liberating Spirit in its
tracks, the Spirit blows, of course, where it wills.

Exactly fifty years ago in 1956 it whipped up a considerable
storm with the appearance of a book which was talked about
across the globe. Trevor Huddleston's Naught for your comfort,
which my parents gave me when I was eight or nine, was the very
first religious book that I read. It seems perhaps somewhat dated
now. A little paternalistic in places. A product, for sure, of its time.
But how its pages nonetheless still sparkle with the Spirit's presence. The spirit of God bringing good news to the poor and
freedom for the oppressed through the ministry of a courageous
Anglican priest amidst the seeming hopelessness of apartheid
South Africa's scrap-heaps and shanty towns.

I'll never forget the impression that Trevor Huddleston's stories
of horror, hope and healing made on me. He said he had nothing
to say that was comforting, only challenging. But in the challenge
he comforted – and confirmed me – in the conviction that the Gospel could make a difference to people's lives. And the story that
most did this for me – perhaps because as a fledgling musician I
could identify with it myself – was the story of a little boy, Hugh,
lying sick in bed, who, when Fr Trevor asked what would most
make him better, said that he'd like to learn the trumpet because
he wanted to be the next Louis Armstrong, Duke Ellington or
Dizzy Gillespie, a request which saw Hugh receive a gleaming
trumpet just days later.

Would we have taken that request very seriously? Or would we
have simply dismissed it as just another hopeless dream – cyni-
cally adding, perhaps, that the little boy would probably sell the

trumpet anyway the moment he recovered. Which of us would really have been attuned, as was Trevor Huddleston, to the look of determination in those young eyes? Would we have grasped the underlying truth, that jazz and justice are but two sides of the same very thin coin, since in the melodic freedom of jazz to which the little boy was drawn – its reliance on the improvised and the spontaneous – the boy was actually discovering his community's deepest desire for freedom? Would we have rushed out immediately to buy that trumpet?

'Always act on impulse,' Trevor Huddleston said of that bed-side encounter and its aftermath. And he was right. Because the consequence of buying that trumpet was that the little boy who received it – Hugh Masekela – became one of the world's greatest jazz trumpeters.

'The Spirit of the Lord is upon me', Jesus says in his home synagogue, as he reads in public for the very first time, choosing words from Isaiah's writings. 'For he has anointed me to bring good news to the poor … to proclaim the year of the Lord's favour'. He closes the scroll and adds – in one of history's most significant throw-away lines – 'Today this scripture is fulfilled in your hearing'.

When Trevor Huddleston gave a trumpet to Hugh Masekela the Spirit of the Lord brought fulfilment to a little boy's dreams which would soon be heard by everyone around him. And it is this same Spirit which is upon each and every one of us; the liberating Spirit that is good news for our communities, the transforming Spirit which fulfils our deepest hopes in ways which are sometimes beyond our imagining and understanding, and most often completely unexpected. Thanks be to God.

Choir and trumpet: The Spirit is moving, Galloway

Creed, The Dean:

Let us declare our faith in the God who moves us to work for freedom.

We believe in God the Father,
from whom every family
in heaven and on earth is named.
We believe in God the Son,
who lives in our hearts through faith,
and fills us with his love.

We believe in God the Holy Spirit,
who strengthens us
with power from on high.

We believe in one God;
Father, Son and Holy Spirit.
Amen.

Solo soprano: Spirit of holiness, wisdom and faithfulness
wind of the Lord blowing strongly and free:
strength of our serving and joy of our worshipping –
Spirit of God, bring your fulness to me.

Intercessions, Jacqui Mallinson:

Let us pray.

Spirit of Holiness,
bless your people throughout the world,,
fill your Church with compassion and love,
anoint us as your disciples
to bring good news to the poor,
to challenge injustice in our homes, or where we live and work,
to proclaim release to all who are shackled by sin
      or circumstance.

Spirit of Wisdom,
bless all leaders in local and national government,
in Churches and faith communities everywhere.
Fill them with integrity and commitment,

to unite all people for the common good,
to promote respect for difference,
to cast out fear and prejudice.

Spirit of Faithfulness,
bless all who are estranged or lost,
those who lack opportunity or hope:
the asylum seeker and the homeless,
the sick, the unemployed and those who mourn.
Fill them with the gentle breeze of your presence,
that the hope of the scriptures may be fulfilled in their hearing.

Solo soprano: Spirit of holiness, wisdom and faithfulness
wind of the Lord blowing strongly and free:
strength of our serving and joy of our worshipping –
Spirit of God, bring your fulness to me.

Peace, The Dean:
God has made us one in Christ.
He has set his seal upon us and, as a pledge of the fulness that
 is to come,
has given the Spirit to dwell in our hearts. Alleluia.
The peace of the Lord be always with you:
And also with you.

The Dean:
Let us offer one another a sign of peace.

Choir Offertory song: Ev'ry time I feel the Spirit, Bob Chilcott

Eucharistic Prayer, The Dean:
The Lord is here.
His Spirit is with us.
Lift up your hearts.
We lift them to the Lord.
Let us give thanks to the Lord our God.
It is right to give thanks and praise.

Father, we give you thanks and praise
through your beloved Son Jesus Christ, your living Word,
through whom you have created all things;
who was sent by you in your great goodness to be our Saviour.
By the power of the Holy Spirit he took flesh;
as your Son, born of the blessed Virgin,
he lived on earth and went about among us;
he opened wide his arms for us on the cross;
he put an end to death by dying for us;
and revealed the resurrection by rising to new life;
so he fulfilled your will and won for you a holy people.
And now we give you thanks
that, after he had ascended far above all heavens,
and was seated at the right hand of your majesty,
he sent forth upon the universal Church
your holy and life-giving Spirit;
that through his glorious power the joy of the everlasting
Gospel might go forth into all the world.

Therefore with angels and archangels,
and with all the company of heaven,
we proclaim your great and glorious name,
for ever praising you and singing:

Choir: Sanctus and Benedictus, Bob Chilcott

Lord, you are holy indeed, the source of all holiness;
grant that by the power of your Holy Spirit,
and according to your holy will,
these gifts of bread and wine
may be to us the body and blood of our Lord Jesus Christ;

who, in the same night that he was betrayed,
took bread and gave you thanks;
he broke it and gave it to his disciples, saying:
Take, eat; this is my body which is given for you;
do this in remembrance of me.

216

In the same way, after supper
he took the cup and gave you thanks;
he gave it to them, saying:
Drink this, all of you;
this is my blood of the new covenant,
which is shed for you and for many for the forgiveness of sins.
Do this, as often as you drink it,
in remembrance of me.

Great is the mystery of faith:
Christ has died,
Christ is risen,
Christ will come again.

And so, Father, calling to mind his death on the cross,
his perfect sacrifice made once for the sins of the whole world;
rejoicing in his mighty resurrection and glorious ascension,
and looking for his coming in glory,
we celebrate this memorial of our redemption.
As we offer you this our sacrifice of praise and thanksgiving,
we bring before you this bread and this cup
and we thank you for counting us worthy
to stand in your presence and serve you.

Send the Holy Spirit on your people
and gather into one in your kingdom
all who share this one bread and one cup,
so that we, in the company of all the saints,
may praise and glorify you for ever,
through Jesus Christ our Lord;
by whom, and with whom, and in whom,
in the unity of the Holy Spirit,
all honour and glory be yours, almighty Father,
for ever and ever. *Amen.*

Lord's Prayer, The Dean:
Uniting our prayers with those of the Church Universal and remembering that filled with the Spirit the apostles spoke in
different languages, so we say in our own language the prayer that

217

Jesus taught us: *Our Father …*

Fraction, The Dean:
We break this bread
To share in the body of Christ.
Though we are many, we are one body,
Because we all share in the one bread.

Communion during which the Choir sings: Agnus Dei, Bob Chilcott

Prayer after communion, The Dean:
Almighty and everliving God,
who fulfilled the promises of Easter
by sending us your Holy Spirit
and opening to every race and nation
the way of life eternal:
open our lips by your Spirit,
that every tongue may tell of your glory;
through Jesus Christ our Lord. *Amen.*

Farewell, Canon Chivers:
Thank you for joining us in our worship this morning as we've
celebrated the warmth and the joy of the Holy Spirit. As I bid you
farewell from Blackburn Cathedral I ask you to join me in praying
that the Spirit may always be upon each one of us, as together we
seek God's blessing:

Blessing, The Dean:
The Spirit of truth lead us into all truth,
give us grace to confess that Jesus Christ is Lord,
and strengthen you to proclaim the word and works of God;
and the blessing of God Almighty, the Father, the Son and the
Holy Spirit, be among us and remain with us always. *Amen.*

Hymn: Holy Spirit, come confirm us

*Organ Voluntary: Sortie from Messe de la Pentecote, Olivier
Messiaen*

52. The quest for peace

17 September 2006

At ten past eight now it's time for Sunday Worship, which this morning explores how dialogue between different faith perspectives can promote peace. It's introduced by the Dean of Blackburn, The Very Reverend Christopher Armstrong.

Music: My peace I leave you, my peace I give you, Taizé

Welcome, The Dean:
Good morning and welcome to Blackburn Cathedral for this act of worship focussing on peace and coming, of course, in a week which has seen an outpouring of grief and soul-searching around the fifth anniversary of 9/11. A week which has also seen people register anger and incomprehension at remarks made during the course of a lecture by Pope Benedict XVI, which seemed to associate Islam with violence, and on a day when millions around the globe are focussing their prayerful attention on the shattered landscape of war-torn Darfur.

Salaam. Shalom. Peace. In whatever language or cultural context the concept is expressed, peace has proved itself to be one of the most elusive aspirations for human beings to realise. Here in Blackburn, a northern post-industrial town recently described as one of the most 'segregated' places in Britain, we struggle like so many others to bridge the divisions of culture and perception that too often see people leading parallel lives. We do so by attempting to rediscover shafts of light – diamonds in the dust, as it were – of the religious traditions from which our community is composed: Christian, Muslim, Jewish, Hindu, Sikh and Buddhist.

Music: My peace I leave you, my peace I give to you, Taizé

This morning, two representatives of the town's faith communities, Canon Chris Chivers, whose focus here is interfaith relations, and Anjum Anwar, the Education Officer from the Lancashire Council of Mosques, with whom he works to promote dialogue and understanding, are joined by our cathedral musicians and by young people from Blackburn College and our own cathedral community.

Over the past few years since some difficult days for northern towns when racial hatred exploded into violence, the need for dialogue between religions – as also for dialogue between faith communities and secular institutions – has become more pressing. Since 7/7 last year Chris and Anjum have been facilitating and leading public dialogues in this cathedral which we see as a vital meeting place for people of all faiths and none. These conversations in what is widely regarded as the public square of our community promote understanding as they conquer prejudice and fear with respect and emerging friendship, the very qualities which are signs of God's promised kingdom, the longed-for reality about which the writer of our first hymn speaks as he prays: Thy kingdom come, O God, thy rule, O Christ, begin.

Hymn: Thy kingdom come, O God

Prayer and Commentary, Canon Chivers:
Let us pray:
Break the iron rod of human sinfulness, O Lord, take the stubbornness which makes of differences a set of stumbling blocks, and turn these into stepping stones to a new dawn where the Morning Star will be a sign for us of your kingdom of peace and justice. *Amen.*

Breaking the iron rod of human sinfulness, recognising what prevents us from doing so and promoting peace, is never easy: a lesson I was taught very starkly when on a visit with my wife Mary to the United Nations complex in pre-9/11 New York.

It was a beautiful late-Fall afternoon – the golden, red and brown leaves of the trees shimmering in the sunlight. And as we wandered through the sculpture garden which surrounds the UN main building, so Mary took a number of photographs, among which was a series of images of my favourite sculpture. Entitled They shall beat their swords into ploughshares, it was a gift of the Soviet Government during the Cold War years – a fact which is not of course without its considerable ironies. But these aside, it is an amazingly dynamic work which depicts a lone soldier beating his sword into a ploughshare with extraordinary force and determination. As Mary photographed the sculpture, I extolled its beauty and symbolic power. But before I could get too carried away, she interjected: "That's all very well, but look over there". She was pointing towards an enormous advert for Pepsi Cola on the opposite river-bank, as she added: "Isn't that what most people see as the real icon of our times, not this sculpture?"

It's a comment that's stayed with me, not least during these conflict-filled years post 9/11, for as a person of faith living in a world where the tyranny of the market, and its enslavement to self-serving competitiveness, seems to hold such sway, I often wonder if there is anything I can do, anything each one of us can do, to bring a vision of peace to the world through the marketplace of the faiths?

That question strikes at the heart of what it means to be human, and it certainly doesn't mean we need fear for our distinctiveness. But we do have to learn to allow and even to serve difference with profound respect. We hear now a haunting setting of words from Isaiah chapter 2 – the words so powerfully depicted in that New York sculpture – written specially for this morning's worship by our Assistant Director of Music, James Davy.

Choir: And they shall beat their swords into ploughshares, James Davy

Reading, Sara Fergus:
A reading from Isaiah Chapter 2

In days to come
the mountain of the Lord's house
shall be established as the highest of the mountains,
and shall be raised above the hills;
all the nations shall stream to it.
Many peoples shall come and say,
'Come, let us go up to the mountain of the Lord,
to the house of the God of Jacob;
that he may teach us his ways
and that we may walk in his paths.'
For out of Zion shall go forth instruction,
and the word of the Lord from Jerusalem.
He shall judge between the nations,
and shall arbitrate for many peoples;
they shall beat their swords into ploughshares,
and their spears into pruning-hooks;
nation shall not lift up sword against nation,
neither shall they learn war anymore.
O house of Jacob,
come, let us walk
in the light of the Lord!

Commentary, Anjum Anwar:
As a Muslim I certainly share both the vision of peace which that reading from the prophet Isaiah sets as our goal, and the strong sense of our prevalent culture as one that is far too competitive and self-seeking.

What I think is required here is a self-denying, self-sacrificial attitude which for me, is encapsulated in the Quranic story of the Hudaybiya treaty. The prophet Muhammed (peace be upon him) was told in a dream to perform what is called the lesser pilgrimage, a re-enactment of one of prophet Abraham's journeys which involved him leaving Medina and travelling to Mecca. Stopping at a place called Hudaybiya he encountered members of the tribe of the Quraysh who did not want to give him access to Mecca. The Quraysh believed that to let the Prophet and his delegation into their territory would be to surrender their power and influence to the visitors. Potential conflict, however, a conflict which the Muslims would easily have won through sheer numbers, was averted by the Prophet's dialogue with the representatives of the Quraysh, and the treaty which emerged from these conversations, the terms of which allowed him to make a pilgrimage to Mecca the following year without risk of attack.

Though in a position of advantage in terms of power, the Prophet (peace be upon him) saw that such power should be sacrificed for the greater good of the whole region. This would avoid bloodshed and lead to a lasting peace, the kind of peace which injunction after injunction in the Qu'ran calls Muslims to promote.

Reading, Nusheen Siddiqui:
A reading of verses from the Holy Qu'ran, Surra 8 verse 61,
surra 25 verse 63 and surra 5 verse 32

If they incline to peace, you also incline to it.

The worshippers of the All-Merciful are they who tread gently upon the earth, and when the ignorant address them, they reply, "Peace!"

If you save one human life, it is as if you have saved the whole of humanity.

Commentary, Canon Chivers:
These verses from the Qu'ran, a holy book we have honoured before in this cathedral when the wider community have joined our worship, echo a verse in the Jewish book, the Talmud. Like the famous prayer of St Francis of Assisi, they remind us of our responsibility to be channels of peace.

Hymn: Make me a channel of your peace

Reading, Jonathan Turner:
A reading from Revelation chapter 22

Then I saw a new heaven and a new earth; for the first heaven and the first earth had passed away, and the sea was no more. And I saw the holy city, the new Jerusalem, coming down out of heaven from God, prepared as a bride adorned for her husband. And I heard a loud voice from the throne saying,
'See, the home of God is among mortals.
He will dwell with them;
they will be his peoples,
and God himself will be with them;
he will wipe every tear from their eyes.
Death will be no more;
mourning and crying and pain will be no more,
for the first things have passed away.'

Commentary, Canon Chivers:
Those words from the Book of the Revelation have at turns captivated and daunted women and men down the generations. They still do. But if we're honest, we'd have to admit that for all the prayers and hopes of faithful people down the ages we are no closer to seeing the signs of a new heaven and new earth than we were when those words were first written.

Often, in history, religions have rightly been perceived as the stumbling blocks that prevents a shared hope for peace from being realised. So concerned to protect their own territorial or doctrinal integrity, narrowly self-interested and inward-looking, religions have rightly been castigated for causing conflict.

But neither those who have resorted to terrorism in recent years, for example – nor those who have responded with such force – can claim the moral high ground here, least of all in religious or ethical terms. Which is where the voice of real religion has once again begun to come into its own, uniting people across doctrinal and territorial differences to seek God's mercy for destructiveness which is so against God's will, and to be renewed, once again, in the divine call for peace.

Choir: Kyrie from African Sanctus, David Fanshawe

Commentary, Anjum Anwar:
That beautiful, evocative fusion from the African Sanctus by David Fanshawe, bringing together the Islamic call to prayer and the Christian cry that God may have mercy on our sins and failings, can be an inspiration to all of us of whatever faith or worldview to find the meeting places in our thinking and living. I am reminded, for instance, of the occasion when, in order to escape the atrocities being committed on Muslims by the citizens of Mecca, the Prophet Muhammed (peace be upon him) sent his fellow men and women to seek refuge in Abysennia, because, he said, Negas, a Christian king 'rules there with justice'. For the Prophet, it was natural to turn to a Christian king for leadership and friendship. For me, as a Muslim, living with Christians and other people of faith still means security and peace. It has historical roots and is the way forward now.

When I think of this coming together of different traditions, I recall with great sadness a contrasting moment which I experienced myself on 12 September 2001. I walked into a shop that has been serving my family for many years, yet, on the day following 9/11, I was refused service. Even though I was not wearing a head-scarf, and was not thus so readily identifiable in terms of my faith, the people behind the counter knew very well that I was a Muslim. They also knew of my commitment to the community. In their rejection of me, their placement of me alongside those who smashed planes into the towers of the World Trade Centre, I felt that I was being crucified – metaphorically – for my faith. But at one and the same time I also realised that this was happening through fear and ignorance. It showed me in fact the gaps in relationships that I had supposed to be secure and friendly, gaps of understanding I needed to fill by showing people the best of my own faith tradition – and celebrating the best in other traditions – so that people can see the great religions not as forces to be feared but as agents of God's peace in the world. In that moment of rejection I resolved to work with my religious friends and counterparts to be in dialogue with a world which seems to focus only on the worst kinds of religion and rarely to embrace the best of every tradition which is genuinely peace-loving. At this time when Pope Benedict's remarks have reinforced a note of potential suspicion in the relationship between Christians and Muslims, and clearly inflamed tensions around the world, I recall that from my Christian neighbours I hear the divine invitation to 'turn the other cheek', which parallels timely guidance from Sura 28, verse 55 of the Holy Qur'an: 'And when they hear vain talk, they turn away therefrom and say: To us our deeds and to you yours, peace be to you.'

Commentary, Canon Chivers:
To introduce our prayers, Philippa Hyde sings a setting of another of Isaiah's prophetic utterances, set to music by Charles Villers Stanford, as A Song of Peace. Christians see the rod emerging from the stem of Jesse as Jesus Christ, the Prince of Peace. Muslims and Jews would interpret things differently. But all nonetheless would remain united in a longing to see the spirit of the Lord, the spirit of wisdom and understanding achieve that peace which is the hope of all our striving.

Solo: Song of Peace, Chares Villiers Stanford
There shall come forth a rod out of the stem of Jessie, and a branch shall grow out of his roots;
And the spirit of the Lord shall rest upon him, the spirit of wisdom, and understanding, the spirit of counsel and might, the spirit of knowledge, and of the fear of the Lord:
And he shall not judge after the sight of his eyes, Neither reprove after the hearing of his ears;
And with rightness shall he judge the poor, and reprove with equity the meek of the earth;

And He shall smite the earth with the rod of his mouth, and with the breath of his lips shall he slay the wicked.

And righteousness shall be the girdle of his loins, and faithfulness the girdle of his veins.

The wolf also shall dwell with the lamb.

And the leopard shall lie down with the kid, and the calf and the young lion and the fatling together, and a little child shall lead them.

They shall not hurt nor destroy in all my holy mountain:

For the earth shall be full of the knowledge of the Lord as the waters cover the earth.

And in that day there shall be a root of Jessie which shall stand for ensign unto the people and his rest shall be glorious.

Isaiah 11: 1-6, 8-10 (King James Version)

Commentary, Canon Chivers:

Writing a few years ago, the theologian, Hans Kung, said this: 'No peace among the nations without peace among the religions. No peace among the religions without dialogue between the religions. No dialogue between the religions without investigation of the foundation of the religions.'

Prayers, Sara Fergus:

So let us pray for an openness to investigate the foundations of every religion; for a self-critical approach on the part of believers everywhere; for a gentleness and respectfulness when seeking to understand traditions not our own; for a sensitivity in the language by which we describe other faiths; for a determination to know the story and riches of our own faith so as to feel confident that we can be in conversation with those of different world views.

Lord in your mercy:
hear our prayer.

Jonathan Turner:

Let us give thanks to God for the ongoing dialogue both within and between the great faiths of the world; for a willingness not to avoid our distinctiveness or to water-down difference, but to embrace this as the treasure that God has entrusted to us; and let us pray that we may avoid misrepresenting or hurting one another.

Lord in your mercy:
hear our prayer.

Sara Fergus:

Let us remember before God all those places in the world where there is no peace. On this day when our thoughts focus on Darfur, we pray that the affinity between people of faith may serve to strengthen and to promote harmony rather than to prolong conflict, as we use words of Desmond Tutu which are being prayed today by millions across the globe, before the Choir sings another prayer of his, composed by our Director of Music, Richard Tanner.

Nusheen Siddiqui:

We pray for peace in Darfur that those who are causing death and misery will turn away from racism and violence. We pray for an urgent response through action from the international community, that people everywhere will strive to live in peace, tolerance, and respect, no matter what their faith or race – may we gain the wisdom, grace, and generosity of spirit to overcome our differences and live as one.

Lord in your mercy:
hear our prayer.

Choir: A Prayer of Peace, Richard Tanner
Goodness is stronger than evil,
love is stronger than hate,
light is stronger than darkness,
life is stronger than death,
victory is ours through him who loved us.

Desmond Tutu

Canon Chivers:

Let us pray for the coming of God's kingdom of peace in all its fullness as we say together: *Our Father ...*

Hymn: Lord of all hopefulness

Blessing, The Dean:

The peace of God which passes all understanding keep your hearts and minds in the knowledge and love of God and of his Son Jesus Christ our Lord, and the blessing of God Almighty, the Father, the Son and the Holy Spirit, be among you and remain with you always. *Amen.*

Organ Voluntary: Placare Christe Servulis, Marcel Dupré

53. A celebration of global Anglicanism

27 July 2008

Continuity announcement:
BBC Radio 4. The Archbishop of Canterbury Dr Rowan Williams is joined by bishops from across the Anglican Communion now as he preaches for our special Sunday Worship during the Lambeth Conference. The service comes live from St Dunstan's Church Canterbury, and is led by Canon Chris Chivers. It begins as choirs from local parish churches sing a song from Zimbabwe.

Choir music: Jesu tawa pano

Introduction, Canon Chris Chivers:
Jesus, we are here, here for you. That Zimbabwean song introduces our worship this morning from St Dunstan's Church in Canterbury, where Henry II changed into sackcloth to express penitence for his part in Thomas à Becket's death and where the head of St Thomas More is buried, a church that's a short distance from where hundreds of bishops from around the Anglican Communion are meeting now at the University of Kent.

Representatives of the Conference join us to share something of their experience of faith as it's emerged through the study programme for this year's Lambeth Conference, a programme focusing on the identity of Jesus in the 'I am' sayings of John's Gospel.

Anglicanism is a global phenomenon. Its 80 million members are found in 44 regional and national member churches covering 160 countries. It embraces a huge diversity of cultures and languages. But at its heart stands the one who is light, gate and bread of life, through whose identity we hear echoes of the person God calls each of us to be because we discover Jesus is the way, the truth and the life.

Commissioned Hymn: I am the light

I am the Light whose brightness shines
on every pilgrim's way,
and brings to evil's darkest place
the glorious light of day

I am the Gate that leads to life
along the narrow way,
the Shepherd who will tend my sheep
that none are lost or stray.

I am the Well from whose fresh springs
life-giving water flows
and on each side a tree of life
with leaves for healing grows.

I am the Bread, God's gift from heaven,
sent down to satisfy
that hunger which cries out for food,
who eats shall never die.

I am the Vine whose branches grow
uinited in one root;
who dwell in me, and I in them,
shall live and bear much fruit.

I am the Resurrection life,
the power of God whereby
whoever truly trusts in me
shall live and never die.

I am the Way, the Truth, the Life
and truth shall set you free
to seek and find the way to life
and live that life in me.

Robert Willis

Prayer, Presiding Bishop Carlos Touché-Porter, Primate of Mexico:
Almighty God, in whose Word we believe and are baptized;
help us to draw deeply from the waters of your life
that we may know you in our lives,
in our hearts and homes,
our Churches and nations,
and in all whom we seek to serve in your name. *Amen.*

Andrew Clitherow

Commentary, Canon Chivers:
That prayer was offered by Carlos Touché-Porter, Primate of
Mexico, following a hymn with words written specially for today's
service by the Dean of Canterbury, Robert Willis. Switching conti-
nents to Africa, we now hear a reading from John chapter 11, by
Gary Lillibridge, Bishop of West Texas in The Episcopal Church.

Reading, John 11: 17-27, Bishop Gary Lillibridge:

*When Jesus arrived, he found that Lazarus had already been in the
tomb for four days. Now Bethany was near Jerusalem, some two miles
away, and many of the Jews had come to Martha and Mary to console
them about their brother. When Martha heard that Jesus was coming,
she went and met him, while Mary stayed at home. Martha said to
Jesus, 'Lord, if you had been here, my brother would not have died.
But even now I know that God will give you whatever you ask of
him.' Jesus said to her, 'Your brother will rise again.' Martha said to
him, 'I know that he will rise again in the resurrection on the last
day.' Jesus said to her, 'I am the resurrection and the life. Those who
believe in me, even though they die, will live, and everyone who lives*

and believes in me will never die. Do you believe this?' She said to him, 'Yes, Lord, I believe that you are the Messiah, the Son of God, the one coming into the world.'

Commentary, Canon Chivers:
That 'I am' saying is set in the context of great personal tragedy for Jesus. His friend Lazarus has died. He stands weeping in front of his friend's tomb. Jesus is in fact about to call Lazarus into that newness and fullness of life promised to each of us. But resurrection always has its price, a price which is still being paid across the Anglican Communion. Sebastien Bakare, Bishop of Harare knows this only too well. He told me about the cost of discipleship in Zimbabwe.

Recorded testimony from Bishop Bakare:
One Sunday morning, parishioners had come to worship in the usual way, not knowing the police were going to descend on them. And among those worshippers was a woman four months pregnant. When the police came in they forced everyone out during Holy Communion. And this woman really expected the Police to see that she was pregnant but they just went ahead bashing her. She lost the baby and we expected her to say, 'Goodbye, I'll never go again to that parish.' But behold, three weeks later she was there without her baby more determined than ever to give her life for her faith in Jesus Christ. For me that's resurrection. It's something that maybe God gives you in that moment – something you don't choose: extra energy, extra grace to say, 'If this is what my faith is all about, I'll go for it.'

Archbishop Thabo Magkoba, Primate of Southern Africa and choir:
Goodness is stronger than evil, Desmond Tutu/ James Whitbourn

Prayer, Bishop Mouneer Anis, Primate of Jerusalem and the Middle East:
Almighty and everlasting God,
through Jesus Christ
you have taught us how to follow you:

guide us that we may recognise your Spirit
wherever we may find him
that in the company of faithful friends, neighbours and
  strangers
we may continue to learn your way
of peace and reconciliation. *Amen.*

Andrew Clitherow

Commentary, Canon Chivers:
That prayer, offered by Mouneer Anis, Bishop of the diocese of
Egypt and Primate of Jerusalem and the Middle East, followed a
sung prayer by James Whitbourn, setting words of former Archbishop of Cape Town, Desmond Tutu, which were read by Thabo
Makgoba, the present Archbishop. Both prayers remind us that
whilst the call to discipleship is often lived out in contexts like contemporary Harare where there is considerable conflict and massive
injustice, the ultimate victory of the cross is nonetheless assured.
Yet how each of us can deny that cross, do others an injustice by
the way in which we so often judge our neighbours and on the
basis of such judging all too quickly deny their humanity. Sadly, as
Jesus demonstrated by the number of the times he had to address
this tendency; it can be the religious insiders who are at fault the
most.

Reading, John 8: 2-12, Bishop Kay Goldsworthy, Australia:

*Early in the morning Jesus came again to the temple. All the people
came to him and he sat down and began to teach them. The scribes and
the Pharisees brought a woman who had been caught in adultery; and
making her stand before all of them, they said to him, 'Teacher, this
woman was caught in the very act of committing adultery. Now in the
law Moses commanded us to stone such women. Now what do you
say?' They said this to test him, so that they might have some charge
to bring against him. Jesus bent down and wrote with his finger on
the ground. When they kept on questioning him, he straightened up
and said to them, 'Let anyone among you who is without sin be the
first to throw a stone at her.' And once again he bent down and wrote*

*on the ground. When they heard it, they went away, one by one, be-
ginning with the elders; and Jesus was left alone with the woman
standing before him. Jesus straightened up and said to her, 'Woman,
where are they? Has no one condemned you?' She said, 'No one, sir.'
And Jesus said, 'Neither do I condemn you. Go your way, and from
now on do not sin again.' Again Jesus spoke to them, saying, 'I am the
light of the world. Whoever follows me will never walk in darkness
but will have the light of life.'*

Commentary, Canon Chivers:
As that reading by Kay Goldsworthy, Assistant Bishop of Perth
in Australia reminds us, it's always better to light a candle than to
curse the darkness, for it's into the darkness that any tendency to
stone-throwing should of course be consigned since each of us
falls short of the glory of God. This is why the ministry of millions
of Anglicans who hold a candle up, so that someone else won't
have to stumble, is so inspiring. Two bishops, Roger Bird, Bishop
of Sao Paulo in Brazil, and Dinis Singulane, Bishop of Lebombo in
Mozambique told me stories of lives turned right round in their
contexts. Bishop Roger, first, on the work of his cathedral.

Recorded testimony, Bishop Roger Bird:
They have opened two crèches at St Paul's Cathedral in the
worst favella or slum areas. Before we had these crèches the kids
were either locked up in their houses – and quite often a six year
old would be responsible for the three or four smaller brothers and
sisters – or left to go out into the streets. Now the mothers take the
children there as they go off to work in the morning. They know
the children are now in a safe and clean environment. The children
receive two main meals and two snacks everyday, a lot of education starting wih the three Rs, going through to Religious
education, personal hygiene. The effect of this has been absolutely
incredible and they are clean, loved and happy.

Recorded testimony, Bishop Dinis Singulane:
Swords into ploughshares is a biblical concept of disarmament
which the churches in Mozambique adopted after the end of the

war to invite people to bring their guns. The first thing we do is to make them unusable. And then in exchange we give an instrument of production. There was a soldier who, after being demobilised, kept his gun and he was doing some awful things. His wife stole her husband's gun, brought it to us. In exchange, we gave her a sewing machine. A week after that the husband was asking, 'I want my gun so that I go and get some money.' And she said, 'I can give you money. With that sewing machine I made a wedding dress. How much money were you going to get with your gun?' And she gave him double the money and the whole family rejoiced that they have found a new way, abandoning guns and earning their living through a decent and honest way of life.

Hymn: Brother, sister, let me serve you

Prayer, Archbishop Paul Kwong, Primate of Hong Kong:
Almighty God and Father,
who breathed your life into humanity
and wrote our names in the dust:
help us to accept the transient nature
of our saintliness and sinfulness,
that enlightened by the witness of your Son,
we may find and ever hold fast
to the eternity of your love. *Amen.*

Andrew Clitherow

Commentary, Canon Chivers:
To hold fast to the eternity of divine love, as Paul Kwong, Archbishop of Hong Kong reminded us in that prayer, to turn that love outwards into care for neighbour and stranger alike, to ensure, in the words of St Ireaneus that the glory of God is human beings fully alive, this is perhaps the greatest challenge of an age when cynicism and despair seems to reign. It's easier of course to succumb to the many fears that stalk us, or that seem to hem us in on every side. Much more costly, as Raphael Hess, Bishop of

Saldhana Bay, in Southern Africa, reminds us in our Gospel reading, to confront fear itself.

Choir Music: Gospel Alleluia

Gospel Reading, John 6: 16-20, Bishop Raphael Hess, Saldhana Bay, Southern Africa:
When evening came, his disciples went down to the lake, got into a boat, and started across the lake to Capernaum. It was now dark, and Jesus had not yet come to them. The lake became rough because a strong wind was blowing. When they had rowed about three or four miles, they saw Jesus walking on the lake and coming near the boat, and they were terrified. But he said to them, 'It is I – the Greek can be translated, I am – do not be afraid.'

Choir Music: Alleluia

Sermon, Archbishop Rowan Williams:
All three of our Bible readings this morning show us people who suddenly find themselves helpless and threatened. Jesus' friends on board ship are at risk of drowning as an unexpected storm hits them. The woman dragged before Jesus is not only at risk of being lynched, her shame and guilt are exposed in front of everyone – and this in a society like many that still exist today where 'social death' is almost as frightening as literal death for women who lose their honour. And Mary and Martha are left stranded and disoriented by bereavement – probably for most of us the experience that is most likely to knock us sideways and leave us, like Mary and Martha, lost for words, tempted to look around for someone to blame, maybe none too sure about what we believe.

And in all these stories of threats and insecurities, Jesus doesn't instantly solve all the problems as if with a magic wand. First he simply tells people that he's there, and the fact that he's there begins to make the difference. Even before he opens the grave and brings Lazarus back to life, he tells Martha, 'Where I am, there is always new life'. When the sinful woman is brought to him, he initially says nothing; when the woman is left alone with him, she only has to look and listen, and she knows that there is hope for her: the hostile, merciless shouts have fallen silent, and in that silence her heart can expand and her soul come back to life. And for the disciples in the storm-tossed boat, the first thing they hear is, 'It is I': I am here, and as long as I am here there is something greater and deeper than your fear of danger.

So much of what we've heard about in our service this morning has been about situations of threat and helplessness; and we've heard from some of our brothers and sisters who witness in these places as part of a church that is by no means powerful. It may be a minority in a non-Christian setting, or it may be a tiny presence in a much bigger Christian spectrum, or it may be harassed and deprived of resources and security. These are not churches that can solve problems by their wealth and influence – though it's extraordinary just how much these small or poor churches do achieve in reconciliation and empowerment.

But all of them seek simply to do and say what Jesus did – He's here they say. 'We're here to tell you that he's here; and if he's here, then whatever it may feel like, you're not alone and you're not trapped.'

This Conference is a time when we can tell each other – and tell the world – about this first and most important job that Anglicans, like other Christians, do: being there, so that they can say 'Christ is here; you're not alone.' They say it where there is daily terror and death, where large communities know levels of daily bereavement we can't imagine – in Sudan and Zimbabwe and the Philippines and Sri Lanka; where populations starve or are driven from their homes, where those who struggle for justice and honesty may be abducted and killed. They say it where generations are being wiped out through the HIV/AIDS pandemic – where many, especially women, bear the load not only of poverty and disease but public stigma as well. They say it where Christians are threatened by storms of prejudice and violence among non-Christian neighbours. And they say it too where people who seem to be comfortable and at ease begin to face their own inner chaos and wonder what they really believe and whether there's anything or anyone they can trust.

Last week, at one of the morning services at the Conference, one of our African bishops spoke powerfully about how Jesus himself is the gift, even before he does anything, heals or feeds anyone, and, he said, we have to ask, 'What if the Church itself is the gift, the sign of something new and life giving, even before it solves any problems, brings peace or prosperity or education or medicine?'

It's a very good question. And if we want to answer that, yes, the Church itself really is the gift, then the Church has to look like a gift. It has to look like a solace where people don't seem to be alone or trapped, anxious and fearful: a place where people seem to live in a larger more joyous and hopeful atmosphere, and where they are treasured and nourished as precious images of God.

Churches that are divided and fearful and inward-looking don't easily give that message; and our Anglican family badly needs to find some ways of resolving its internal tensions that will set it free to be more confidently what God wants it to be. Part of our agenda at this Conference is to do with this. But our willingness to work at it constructively has a lot to do with hearing good news from our own members – the sort of good news we've heard something of this morning. As our brothers and sisters from these places of conflict and crisis remind us of how they daily try to be a real gift to their neighbours, assuring them that they're not alone and not trapped, they remind all of us in the Anglican family that when we feel helpless, storm-tossed or bereaved as we think about our Church conflicts, Jesus is here with us too, saying, 'Where I am there is life. I don't condemn you. Don't be afraid. I am here.'

We'll be praying, then, that God will help us sort out some of our tensions as we listen to this good news – so that we can go on saying it with joy and conviction to the world around. Men and women here and worldwide live in different kinds of helplessness – it may be through poverty and disease, it may be through personal loss or doubt or pain or shame. But in all these circumstances, the one thing we know is that the life and the love of God in Jesus are never absent. We may not see it all at once, but there is a door out of the prison into a new world, a holy world, where healing and mercy can hold us.

Choir Anthem: This sanctuary of my soul, Charles Wood

This sanctuary of my soul
unwitting I keep white and whole,
unlatched and lit, if Thou should'st care
to enter or to tarry there.

With parted lips and outstretched hands
and listening ears Thy servant stands,
call Thou early, call Thou late,
to Thy great service dedicate.

Commentary, Canon Chivers:
This sanctuary of my soul, words from the poem Expectans
Expectavi by Charles Hamilton Sorley to music by Charles Wood,
which takes us into our prayers. These are led by Ingrid Chien
from Taiwan, Samuel Dow from Australia, Nontuthuko Chamane
from South Africa, Luiz Coehlo from Brazil, and Fr Michael
Sniffen from The Episcopal Church, who are among the sixty
young Anglican stewards at the Conference.

Ingrid Chien:
We give thanks for the witness to Christ of Anglicans across the
centuries: for that fullness of life received through prayer, study of
the scriptures, the sacraments and care for neighbour and stranger.
May all be blessed in our age with the vision and imagination of
the one who says, I am the resurrection and the life.

Samuel Dow:
We pray for all this day who live in fear of war, famine or persecution, for those afraid of others or of what lurks within
themselves. May each know the presence of the one who says I
am, do not be afraid.

Nontuthuko Chamane:
We pray for those who suffer the darkness of oppression, violence, addiction or isolation, for all hemmed in by suffering or sin. May everyone know the warmth and brightness of the one who says I am the light of the world.

Luiz Coehlo:
We give thanks for the rich diversity of the Anglican Communion, for our ecumenical and interfaith partners, and for everyone of goodwill. As we acknowledge differences of context and perspective, of tradition and understanding, may all seek even amidst division the fullness of the one who says I am the way, the truth and the life.

Collect, Fr Michael Sniffen:
Lord God, who came to the disciples by night
and brought them to safety,
we thank you that you have called us to lead others
through hazardous times:
grant us strength and gentleness,
wisdom and grace,
that in the company of Christ
we may uphold the tradition of faith we have inherited
and amidst the darkness of our present age,
may celebrate that communion of mutual understanding
and respect which you have called us to share with others.
Amen.

Andrew Clitherow

Canon Chivers:
Uniting our prayers with those of the Church universal so we say in our own language the prayer that Jesus taught us: *Our Father...*

As we look for our identity in the one who is bread of life, door, light, shepherd and life, so we sing the Indian hymn: Jesus the Lord said: I am.

241

Hymn: Jesus the Lord said, I am the bread...

Blessing: Archbishop of Canterbury

Sunday Worship came live from St Dunstan's in Canterbury. The preacher was the Archbishop of Canterbury, Dr Rowan Williams and the leader was Canon Chris Chivers. The choirs were directed by James Whitbourn, the organist was Stephen Barker, and the producer was Philip Billson.

54. Marking Anne Frank's 80th birthday

14 June 2009

Continuity announcement:
BBC Radio 4. Last Friday was the 80th anniversary of Anne Frank's birth. Today's Sunday Worship from Blackburn Cathedral is a meditation on her life and legacy, using extracts from her diary set to music by James Whitbourn in his oratorio, Annelies. The leader is Canon Chris Chivers.

Instrumental music: from the Introit, Annelies

Introduction, Canon Chris Chivers:
Good morning and welcome to this meditation commemorating the eightieth birthday of a person forever trapped in our imaginations as a teenaged girl. The name Anne Frank is emblazoned across the twentieth century; her diary – read by almost as many people as the Bible – a witness to all that is both best and most bestial in human nature. It's strange to think that Anne was from the same generation as Her Majesty The Queen, and that she had a newspaper photo of the then Princess Elizabeth on the wall of the attic bedroom in Amsterdam in which she and her family, and a group of their friends, hid from the Nazis for over two years. Terrifying to reflect that save for her father, Otto, betrayal led their lives to be extinguished amidst the horrors of Auschwitz and Belsen. Anne's story is part of an appalling period in human history, a period in which the lives of millions were senselessly destroyed. A Jewish girl persecuted for no other reason than who she was: but one whose capacity to hope resonates down the corridors of time, as it transcends the barriers by which people seek to limit the way they define themselves and others. Our opening prayer is led by the Dean of Blackburn, Christopher Armstrong.

Prayer, The Very Reverend Christopher Armstrong, Dean of Blackburn:
Lord of all nations and faiths, as we worship in freedom this morning, hear our prayer for all who live imprisoned by fear or anxiety, that the words and music we offer may inspire in them a new hope for liberation, the hope offered in the prayer that you taught us: *Our Father ...*

Commentary, Canon Chivers:
The composer James Whitbourn was the first to be allowed to set parts of Anne Frank's diary as an oratorio, Annelies. With his librettist Melanie Challenger, he's woven extracts into a concert-length narrative – with passages in English, Dutch and German – the contours of which we follow in this meditation.

In this way, Anne's words are transported on wings of song. As Elie Wiesel, the Auschwitz survivor reminds us, music can take us to the world's highest palaces and its darkest prisons.

We hear first Anne's description of the family's plans to go into hiding.

Music: Movement 3, The plan to go into hiding

When would we go into hiding?
Where would we hide?
In the city? In the country? In a house? In a shack?

8 July 1942

These questions kept running through my mind.
I started packing my important belongings.
The first thing was my diary.
Memories mean more to me than dresses.

8 July 1942

Ik zal, hoop ik, aan jou alles kunnen toevertrouwen, zoals ik het nog aan niemand gekund heb, en ik hoop dat je een grote steun voor me zult zijn.

I will, I trust, be able to confide everything to you, as I understand it, and I hope you will be a great support to me.

12 June 1942

It seems like years since Sunday morning.
So much has happened,
it's as if the whole world had
suddenly turned upside down.

8 July 1942

Commentary, Canon Chivers:
'So much has happened; the world has turned upside down.'
It's hard to imagine what it must be like to abandon your home
and possessions and be propelled towards an unknown and totally fear-filled future. But someone who's experienced this from
the inside is Thea Hurst, who as a young Jewish girl, Thea Gersten
from Leipzig, had to forsake her home first for Poland and then for
the United Kingdom, leaving her father to his eventual death in
Treblinka. Like Anne Frank, Thea kept a diary – hers from 1939 to
1947. Published in German, it will soon be available in English.
Thea told me something of the genesis of the diary.

Recorded testimony, Thea Gersten:
In the beginning of 1939 when there was chaos without and
within, I decided to write a diary because my best friend had left,
my family had left, my cousins had gone, my father was gone, my
mother was busy, so I decided I needed to keep and tell someone.
And for the next eight years my diary became my constant companion. I began to wrestle with, 'Who is God, and why is God
allowing this to happen?' I had been seeing God in a very immature a childish way. I wrestled with it for many pages in my diary.
And I came to the conclusion that I had to see God in a very different light. And I end my diary actually by saying I need to love and
show understanding to everyone I meet. That is my religion today.

Music (tolling bell motif) from Movement Five: Life in hiding

Commentary, Canon Chivers (over music):
One of the most remarkable features of Anne Frank's diary is the way fear seems always to be met and overcome by hope. During the day she hears the constant chimes of the Westertoren Clock – emphasising the monotony of life in the attic – yet in the dead of night the same sound brings such reassurance.

Hope and fear. It's a combination that's a strong feature of Jewish responses from within the horrors of Holocaust, as the prayer we'll now hear reminds us. Scratched by a Jewish prisoner on the walls of a cell in Cologne during the Second World War, it introduces Psalm 46, an expression of hope for a world transformed by the goodness of God.

Prayer, Emily Crewe:
I believe in the sun, even when I cannot see it.
I believe in love, even when I cannot feel it.
I believe in God, even when he is silent.

Psalm 46, Rachel Fielding:
God is our refuge and strength, a very present help in trouble;
Therefore we will not fear, though the earth be moved, and
though the mountains tremble in the heart of the sea;
Though the waters rage and swell, and though the mountains
quake at the towering seas.
There is a river whose streams make glad the city of God, the
holy place of the dwelling of the Most High.
God is in the midst of her; therefore shall she not be removed;
God shall help her at the break of day.
The nations are in uproar and the kingdoms are shaken,
but God utters his voice and the earth shall melt away.
The Lord of hosts is with us; the God of Jacob is our stronghold.
Come and behold the works of the Lord, what destruction he
has wrought upon the earth.
He makes wars to cease in all the world; he shatters the bow
and snaps the spear and burns the chariots in the fire.
'Be still, and know that I am God; I will be exalted among the

nations; I will be exalted in the earth.'
The Lord of hosts is with us; the God of Jacob is our stronghold.

Music from Movement Five:

One day this terrible war will be over,
and we'll be people again,
and not just Jews.

11 April 1944

Canon Chivers:
"People again and not just Jews". This telling assertion points
to Anne Frank's unshakeable confidence in the humanity which
others sought to deny in her, as also to her implicit trust in God.
Gillian Walnes, director of the Anne Frank Trust, tells us now
where she feels this quality in Anne came from, and her thoughts
on Anne's living legacy.

Recorded testimony, Gillian Walnes:
She writes in her diary, "If God let's me live I will not remain
insignificant I will go into the world and help mankind". The irony
is that she died in the most terrible circumstances. We see Anne
Frank as a bright, precocious, in many ways ordinary but in many
ways extraordinary teenager with such a lot to give in her adult
years. But to Nazi ideology she was subhuman, she was consid-
ered not worthy of the right to live. Anne Frank gives us a sense of
what it feels like to be hated for your religion, your race, the colour
of your skin, for anything that's different. We know that by focusing on the story of one teenager whose fears, whose concerns and
hopes for the future are the same as all other teenagers they can
get a greater understanding of the value of human rights and a
compassionate society. She speaks to young people wherever they
are.

Music from Movement 5:

You no doubt want to hear
what I think of life in hiding?

11 July 1942

The blue sky, the bare chestnut tree,
glistening with dew,
the seagulls, glinting with silver
swooping through the air.
As long as this exists,
this sunshine and this cloudless sky,
how can I be sad?

23 February 1944

Commentary, Canon Chivers:
The blue sky, the sunshine, the chestnut tree glistening with
dew: as long as Anne was connected to nature by the things she
could glimpse through the attic window of the secret annex, she
could be hopeful. But the flip side of life in such cramped circumstances – people physically and emotionally tumbling over each
other, the daily fear of discovery: this side of life in the attic must
have been very trying. Yet it was, as Anne recognised, luxury
compared to the hell that people were being consigned to in the
outside world, rounded up, herded into cattle trucks and dis-
patched with such order and precision to almost certain death. It's
impossible to understand what Hannah Arendt, in her famous account of Adolf Eichmann's trial, described as the 'banality of evil'.
When Christians and Jews came to reflect together on the Holocaust – and especially on the part that so-called Christian
civilisation had played in its creation – the strands were recognised to be so complex that only through shared silence could they
be addressed.

Perhaps, in this sense, the sacred space of the music that we hear now, offers us the opportunity to express our own feelings prayerfully and reflectively, as in the traditional plea for divine mercy, Kyrie eleison, we hear the cries of perpetrators and victims alike, surely re-echoed now by those in our world in places of desperate need and suffering pleading for us to do something.

Music: Movement 8, Sinfonia (Kyrie):

Kyrie eleison.

Greek liturgical

Help us. Rescue us from this hell.

27 November 1943

We must be brave and trust in God.

11 April 1944

Commentary, Canon Chivers:
Invitations to put our trust in God can sound so hollow until the moment we actually experience the need to trust, and find it answered not so much by some spectacular act of divine intervention but through the compassion and care offered by our neighbours. Anjum Anwar is Blackburn Cathedral's dialogue development officer – she, a Muslim, and I, a Christian: together we work to build relationships across communities. Anjum was the coordinator of the Anne Frank exhibition when it came to Blackburn last year.

Recorded testimony, Anjum Anwar MBE:
When we were organising the Anne Frank exhibition we knew that one of the biggest challenges we faced would be how to engage the Muslim community. Canon Chivers and myself were in Jerusalem. We picked up a book called BESA which is an Albanian

code of honour. The book is about Albanian Muslims who saved Jews from the Holocaust during the Second World War at the risk of their own lives and their villages. This is a wonderful story that we thought could link the Muslim community to Anne Frank's story. So what we did with this was to create a very small side exhibition to get Muslims to engage with the Jewish story through Anne Frank. And we didn't look back. It was the most wonderful experience to see and for children to accept that this is the story of a fourteen year old child persecuted for her faith, and today in the world we're seeing so many children persecuted for their faith.

Music: from Movement 12, The Hope and the Awakening:

Ich danke dir für all das Gute und Liebe und Schöne.

7 March 1944

Commentary, Canon Chivers:
Ich danke dir für all das Gute und Liebe und Schöne. I thank you God for all that's good, and lovely and beautiful. I'll always remember standing with a group of 8 to 13 year old choristers in the middle of the Anne Frank House in Amsterdam trying to do just that. They'd been rehearsing for a concert and during a break, we visited the House. A noisy group of choirboys, letting off steam, soon became as wide-eyed and reflective a group as you could imagine.

Up the stairs we went, and found ourselves in Anne Frank's bedroom. The boys looked at the newspaper cuttings and pictures on the wall, and gazed out of the window. And then suddenly it happened: we were all helplessly in tears. We didn't need to say why – and we didn't say why – we just knew why.

I met one of those boys a while back, and one of the first things he said to me was "D'you remember when we went to the Anne Frank House?" And of course I did. "For me," he said, "it was one of the most important moments in my life. Anne Frank wanted to be the best writer she could be. She wanted the best from life, the best for other people. She got the worst in return. She was hated for who she was. But she beat them all and became the best ever ... the most successful diarist the world's ever known. I decided I'd do the same and be the best I could be." Today that boy is one of the world's finest musicians.

Short Reading and Prayers, The Very Reverend Chrstopher Armstrong:
Behold, I have set before you this day life and prosperity, death and adversity: choose life.

Deuteronomy 30: 15, 19

Let us pray.

For all who live in the shadow of conflict and the fear that it engenders, especially for the peoples of Iran and North Korea.

For all who suffer persecution on the basis of their faith, ethnicity, sexuality, gender or political conviction.

For all who are powerless casualties of the decisions made by those who exercise power, especially children and young people imprisoned by poverty, neglect or abuse.

Commentary, Canon Chivers:
As our meditation draws to a close let's make these words of Anne Frank's our own prayer for integrity and purity.

Music: Anne's Meditation

Reading, from Anne Frank's diary, Emily Crewe (over the music then sung):

I see the world being slowly
turned into wilderness.

I hear the approaching thunder,
that one day will destroy us too.
And yet, when I look at the sky,
I feel that everything
will change for the better.

15 July 1944

Whenever you feel lonely or sad,
try going to the loft
on a beautiful day and looking
at the sky.
As long as you can look
fearlessly at the sky,
you'll know you're pure within.

23 February 1944

Closing continuity announcement:
Anne's meditation, from James Whitbourn's oratorio, *Annelies*,
ending this morning's Sunday Worship which came from
Blackburn Cathedral. The music was performed by members of
the Northern Chamber Orchestra conducted by Richard Tanner
with soprano soloist Nicola Howard and Blackburn's Renaissance
Singers. The leader was Canon Chris Chivers and the producer
Simon Vivian.

55. Faith in suburbia

20 November 2011

Continuity announcement:
And now Sunday Worship – a celebration for the Feast of Christ the King from John Keble Church, in north London. The service is led by the curate, the Reverend Stephen Young, and the preacher who also introduces the service is the Vicar, Canon Chris Chivers. It begins with the Introit, Moto umewaka leo, God's fire is burning in my soul.

Choir: Moto umewaka leo, God's fire is burning in my soul

Welcome. Canon Chris Chivers, Vicar:
God's fire is burning in my soul. That song from East Africa introduces our worship this morning. You might think it's an unexpected place to start. But then again suburbia these days never quite conforms to the stereotypes people hold.

North London to most perhaps conjures up an image of classic middle-England: shears clipping privet and the twitching of net curtains. Like all stereotypes there's some truth in it – at least historically. But whereas when the church was consecrated exactly seventy-five years ago it served a monochromely white, commuter suburb, now the diversity is amazing. At Deansbrook, the primary school across the road, forty-six first languages are spoken by parents and learners. Here at the church we have worshippers drawn from across Africa, Asia and Europe.

The Reverend Steven Young, Presider and Assistant Curate, continues:
Today, on the feast of Christ the King it's this global nature of his rule and reach that we acknowledge and the stories of our suburb's citizen's reveal this. Like the first apostles, Christians gather together because we're called now to be bearers of God's love for the whole world.

Gospel Reading, Matthew 28: 16-20, Ebere Ikerionwu:

A reading from Matthew chapter 28

*Now the eleven disciples went to Galilee, to the mountain
to which Jesus had directed them. When they saw him, they
worshipped him; but some doubted. And Jesus came and said
to them, 'All authority in heaven and on earth has been given
to me. Go therefore and make disciples of all nations, baptizing
them in the name of the Father and of the Son and of the Holy
Spirit, and teaching them to obey everything that I have
commanded you. And remember, I am with you always, to
the end of the age.'*

Presider:
So we pray for grace to learn how to join in God's mission to
the world as we sing the hymn, Christ is the king, O friends rejoice

Hymn: Christ is the King

Penitence, Presider:
God calls us to light new lamps of faith and offer new hope to
the world. Mindful of the ways in which we fail to be his witnesses
we seek his love and mercy, as we confess our sins.

*Lord God and King of the universe, we have sinned against you, our
neighbours, and the whole of your creation. We are heartily sorry and we
repent. Have mercy on us and bring us to new life in Christ. Amen.*

Absolution, Presider:
May the God who reigns over the whole earth, bring us back to
himself, forgive us our sins, and assure us of his eternal love in
Jesus Christ our Lord. *Amen.*

Presider:
Blessed is the king who comes in the name of the Lord. Peace in
heaven and glory in the highest.

Choir and congregation: Gloria, John Barnard

Collect, Presider:
Let us pray:
God, our Father,
help us to hear the call of Christ the King
and to follow in his service,
whose kingdom has no end;
for he reigns with you and the Holy Spirit,
one God, one glory. *Amen.*

Reading, Genesis 11 1-9, Harry Lamb (Narrator), Daniel Arnell (Voice 1), Eloka Agu (Voice 2):

Narrator: A Reading from Genesis chapter 11
Now the whole earth had one language and the same words. And as they migrated from the east, they came upon a plain in the land of Shinar and settled there. And they said to one another,
Voice 1: 'Come, let us make bricks, and burn them thoroughly.'
Narrator: And they had brick for stone, and bitumen for mortar. Then they said,
Voice 1: 'Come, let us build ourselves a city, and a tower with its top in the heavens, and let us make a name for ourselves; otherwise we shall be scattered abroad upon the face of the whole earth.'
Narrator: The Lord came down to see the city and the tower, which mortals had built. And the Lord said,
Voice 2: 'Look, they are one people, and they have all one language; and this is only the beginning of what they will do; nothing that they propose to do will now be impossible for them. Come, let us go down, and confuse their language there, so that they will not understand one another's speech.'
Narrator: So the Lord scattered them abroad from there over the face of all the earth, and they left off building the city. Therefore it was called Babel, because there the Lord confused the language of all the earth; and from there the Lord scattered them abroad over the face of all the earth.

Sermon, Canon Chris Chivers:

In the name of God: Father, Son and Holy Spirit. Amen.

Anthropologists tell us that every culture has something like a tower of babel myth, a story to explain how that which was created one becomes diverse, and seemingly diffuse as well. At creation, humanity is blessed with one tongue. Adam names all living creatures and this naming is universally understood. But then disaster strikes. The Hebrew Bible legend of babel suggests hubris as the cause. Human beings set out to make themselves like God and they come a cropper. They literally fall flat on their faces. And the consequence of this is a fragmentation, a babble of tongues, the first divide and rule if you like, which preserves divine integrity as it scatters confused humanity in all directions.

It's proved a seductive, if only partially truthful way of understanding what must have been a basic question at the time of the story's telling – 'why are the guys over there different to me?'

But at our mid-week bible study here at the church – a mixed group of people from their twenties to their eighties – we acknowledged it's a baffling and confusing story, as baffling, confusing and fast-moving as has been our experience of suburbia. Seventy-five years ago there seemed to be a unity of culture, ethnicity and life-style choice. Now there's a diversity which at times feels so fragmented as to be completely disorientating.

The story of Babel resonated with our context. But as we came to look beyond the understandable fear that suburban unity has given way to multi-cultural chaos, we began to question the usual reading of the story. For one thing, we noticed from history that if you live by a myth that suggests you should always be getting back to one common spoken language you almost always end up with arrogance. This is the world which supposes that if we imposed English on everyone we would all understand each other. Imagine what nuance would be lost by this. Well don't imagine it, just see it in the impact of global capitalism whose advertising speaks a common language that destroys nuance as it encourages everyone to speak the same acquisitive language, the language that judges us by what we own not who we are, and which the protestors outside St Paul's Cathedral right now are rightly seeking to question. Or we can see it in the retail chains threatening to homogenise our suburban parades of shops.

Our group went back to the text. Perhaps, just perhaps, behind that normative reading of babel as 'unity descended into confusion' lay something else. One of our number noticed that in the previous chapter of Genesis in which the babel story is told humans are already speaking different tongues. So as a seminal moment of disaster shattering unity the story doesn't work in a linear sense. Added to which, the etymology of the word disaster suggests a rain of stars on humanity as much as their fragmentation. Another noticed the way in which most of Genesis is set in the wilderness and the countryside where people meet God on mountains, whereas the editor of the Babel myth is at pains to point-up the city context, and all that the new technology of clay bricks makes possible. Of course technological development can always have negative consequences. But, so another member of the group suggested, might it not be the case that what people were actually doing was to build a ziggurat – those distinctive Bablonian towers about which archeologists get so excited – not as a sign of human wilfulness but as a place to meet God. The rural folk had real mountains. Why couldn't they get the same access to God in the city?

But God had punished them for this, interjected another voice. If we read the story as a punishment for human's over-reaching themselves, an answer to it is given of course in the next chapter of Genesis when God calls Abraham and invites a people to witness to his divine unity of purpose. But what is God's purpose in the multiplicity of tongues? What if God really has some other purpose and the editors of the book have missed it? We found help here from the Jewish tradition of so many of our suburban neighbours, and specifically the writer, George Steiner.

" I felt," he says, "already as a child, that the story of Babel was a 'cover-up'; that it inverted a more ancient and true meaning. Straining to celebrate God's cosmic monarchy," he continues, "the tribes had gathered to build a sublime sky-scraper, a spiralling ascent which could bring their worship closer to his celestial omnipotence. To reward this worshipful labour, the Lord had, albeit in his somewhat brusque and veiled fashion, bestowed on man the incommensurable gift of tongues. He had given men and women the light, the inexhaustible wealth of Pentecost."

The building of the Tower of Babel is then strikingly like the process that led the first white suburbanites in this parish to construct a hut for worship, then a hall, and finally, exactly seventy-five years ago, a church on a hill. Its modernist tower was to be a sign not of human arrogance but of human aspiration and acknowledgement of the divine rule over the whole of creation. It was an act of faith, an investment in human community which has now brought so many languages and cultures into conversation under one roof. The gift of languages in the Babel story then is not punishment – it's not babble – but as Steiner sees it, "blessing without end". Since diversity of language and culture, ethnicity and context, allow truth to be spoken with a depth and range, which one monochromely mother tongue would make impossible. As the second chapter of the Acts of the Apostles suggests, when a monochrome group of citizens is seen in its richness, each speaking in their own tongue, then we discover, that the common language to which their many tongues bear witness, is of course the language of love, which from the first has been the currency of true community.

Reading, Acts 2: 5, 7-11 Pam Perry:
There were devout Jews from eery nation under heaven living in Jerusalem at the time ... they were astonished and amazed. "These are all Galileans aren't they? So how is it that each of us can hear them in our own mother tongues? We can hear them telling us about the powerful things God has done – in our own languages!"

Choir: Jubilate, Charles Villiers Stanford

Creed, Presider:
Let us declare our faith in the God who unites the nations in joyful trust and service.

We believe in God the Father,
from whom every family
in heaven and on earth is named.

We believe in God the Son,
who lives in our hearts through faith,
and fills us with his love.

We believe in God the Holy Spirit,
who strengthens us
with power from on high.

We believe in one God;
Father, Son and Holy Spirit.
Amen.

Presider:
Let us pray that your will may be done on earth, O Lord.

Choir: Mayenziwe 'ntando yakho [Your will be done on earth,
O Lord]

Intercessions, Janet Saffery and Ron South:
As we pray that your will be done on earth as it is in heaven,
we remember all in positions of power,
that they may witness to truth,
govern with integrity
and serve with wisdom.
Your kingdom come:
Your will be done.

We pray for the Church, called to make your reign known
in all the world,
and especially for this parish of John Keble, Mill Hill,
that it may be a place of welcome,
a house of prayer
and a nurturing community,

for all nations and cultures.
Your kingdom come:
Your will be done.

We pray for our neighbours of other faiths, creeds and
world views,
that as we witness to the Lordship of Christ,
and discern your mission in the world,
we may respect the dignity of difference,
embrace our common humanity,
and trust in your saving love for all your children.
Your kingdom come:
Your will be done.

We pray for all whose commitment to the truth of your
kingdom
brings them into conflict with earthly powers,
that they may have patience in tribulation,
courage in danger
and hope in the face of persecution.
Your kingdom come:
Your will be done.

We pray for all who suffer
in body, mind or spirit,
as we ask that each of us may know
God's healing touch in our lives,
and so learn the language of love:
Your kingdom come
Your will be done

Loving God,
you have taught us that the power of the heart
is greater than the power of wealth and might.
Hear us as we pray for the fulfilment of your reign.
We ask this through Jesus Christ our King;
to him be glory and power for ever.
Amen.

Peace, Presider:
To crown all things there must be love,
to bind all together and complete the whole.
Let the peace of Christ rule in our hearts.
The peace of the Lord be always with you
And also with you

Presider:
Let us offer one another a sign of peace.

Offertory Hymn: Let all the world

Eucharistic Prayer, Presider:
The Lord be with you.
And also with you.
Lift up your hearts.
We lift them to the Lord.
Let us give thanks to the Lord our God.
It is right to give thanks and praise.

Father, you made the world and love your creation. You gave your Son Jesus Christ to be our Saviour. His dying and rising have set us free from sin and death. And so we gladly thank you, with saints and angels praising you, and singing:

Sanctus and Benedictus, John Barnard (Choir and Congregation):

We praise and bless you, loving Father, through Jesus Christ, our Lord; and as we obey his command, send your Holy Spirit, that broken bread and wine outpoured may be for us the body and blood of your dear Son.
     On the night before he died he had supper with his friends and, taking bread, he praised you. He broke the bread, gave it to them and said: Take, eat; this is my body which is given for you; do this in remembrance of me.
     When supper was ended he took the cup of wine. Again he praised you, gave it to them and said: Drink this, all of you; this is

my blood of the new covenant, which is shed for you and for many for the forgiveness of sins. Do this, as often as you drink it, in remembrance of me.

So, Father, we remember all that Jesus did, in him we plead with confidence his sacrifice made once for all upon the cross.

Bringing before you the bread of life and cup of salvation, we proclaim his death and resurrection until he comes in glory.

Great is the mystery of faith:
Christ has died
Christ is risen
Christ will come again.

Lord of all life, help us to work together for that day when your kingdom comes and justice and mercy will be seen in all the earth.

Remember your Church throughout the world, make us grow in love, together with Richard and Peter our bishops, and all the clergy. Look with favour on your people, gather us in your loving arms and bring us with the Blessed Virgin Mary, John Keble and all the saints to feast at your table in heaven.

Through Christ, and with Christ, and in Christ, in the unity of the Holy Spirit, all honour and glory are yours, O loving Father, for ever and ever. *Amen.*

Lord's Prayer, Presider:
Uniting our prayers with those of the Church Universal and re-membering the diversity of cultures and languages in our communities, so we say in our own language the prayer that Jesus taught us: *Our Father ... [Fola Adu, Kachi Agu, Gloria Fasuluku and Margaret Attrebi read the Lord's Prayer in their first languages]*

Fraction, Presider:
We break this bread
to share in the body of Christ.
Though we are many, we are one body,
because we all share in the one bread.

Communion during which the Choir sings: Agnus Dei, John Barnard

Prayer after communion, Presider:
Almighty and everliving God,
who fulfilled the promises of Easter
by sending us your Holy Spirit
and opening to every race and nation
the way of life eternal:
open our lips by your Spirit,
that every tongue may tell of your glory;
through Jesus Christ our Lord. *Amen.*

Farewell, Preacher:
Thank you for joining us in our worship this morning as we've celebrated the reign of God in our hearts and lives. As I bid you farewell from John Keble Church, I ask you to join me in praying that we may always be faithful to the truth of God's love as together we seek God's blessing:

Blessing, Presider:
Christ our King make you faithful and strong to do his will, that you may reign with him in glory; And the blessing of God Almighty, the Father, the Son and the Holy Spirit, be among us and remain with us always. *Amen.*

Hymn: Christ triumphant ever reigning

Voluntary: Jubilate, William Mathias